Don't Forgive Too Soon

Extending the Two Hands That Heal

Dennis Linn
Sheila Fabricant Linn
Matthew Linn, S.J.

ILLUSTRATIONS BY FRANCISCO MIRANDA

Paulist Press   New York/Mahwah, N.J.

This book is gratefully dedicated to
Leonard Linn
who, as a father, always forgave us
and now helps us to forgive others.

Acknowledgments

We wish to thank the following persons for their help and loving care in the preparation of the manuscript for this book: Jim, Marie, Jonah & Connor Cox, Rev. Jim Grummer, S.J., Walter Hanss, Dr. Mack Harnden, Dr. Hank & Pat Kankowski, Maria Maggi, Erin & Judy Ryan, Dr. Douglas & Frances Schoeninger, Rev. Robert Sears, S.J., Dr. Len Sperry, Dr. Diana Villegas, Dr. Walter Wink.

Book Design by Saija Autrand, Faces Type & Design.

IMPRIMI POTEST:
D. Edward Mathie, S.J.
Provincial, Wisconsin Province of the Society of Jesus
May 21, 1996

Library of Congress Cataloging-in-Publication Data

Linn, Dennis.
    Don't forgive too soon: extending the two hands that heal / Dennis Linn, Sheila Fabricant Linn, Matthew Linn : illustrations by Francisco Miranda.
        p.   cm.
    Includes bibliographical references.
    ISBN 0-8091-3704-6 (alk. paper)
    1. Forgiveness—Religious aspects—Christianity.   2. Christian life.   I. Linn, Sheila Fabricant.   II. Linn, Matthew.   III. Title.
    BV4647.F55L56   1997
    234'.5—dc21   96-50101
                                                                                      CIP

Published by Paulist Press
997 Macarthur Boulevard
Mahwah, N.J. 07430

Printed and bound in the United States of America

TABLE OF CONTENTS

PREFACE

Most of us know that we should forgive those who hurt us. But how can we forgive when we've tried everything we can think of, including prayer, yet we still feel stuck in a hurt? When we are hurt, most of us are tempted either to be a passive doormat or to strike back and escalate the cycle of violence. We can find more creative responses to hurts by moving through the five stages of forgiveness. The five stages help us extend two hands: one hand that stops the person who hurt us and the other hand that reaches out, calms that person and offers new life.

Over fifteen years ago, two of us (Dennis and Matt) wrote *Healing Life's Hurts*, which is also about the five stages of forgiveness. At that time, we realized that hurts are like small deaths. We discovered that the stages of forgiving someone who has hurt us are the same five stages that Dr. Elisabeth Kübler-Ross observed in her dying patients. Since then, these five stages of forgiveness have received widespread acceptance.

Healing Life's Hurts has sold over four hundred thousand copies in English alone, and has been translated into at least ten foreign languages. The three of us have given hundreds of "Healing Life's Hurts" conferences accredited by professional organizations, such as the American Medical Association, and by various universities. We also have given these conferences to prison inmates and third world villagers with no formal education. After giving conferences on every continent and in over forty countries, we have found that the five stages of forgiveness are universal because they are based upon grieving, which is a fundamental human process.

Although this book is also about the five stages of forgiveness, it is not meant to replace *Healing Life's Hurts*. Each book has a different focus. First, *Healing Life's Hurts* uses more traditional Christian language of grace and prayer and assumes forgiveness to always be a positive emotional and spiritual experience modeled upon Jesus' experience of forgiving on the cross. Our own basic attitude toward forgiveness has not changed: forgiveness is a grace from God. The five stages are simply a way of asking for and opening ourselves to receive God's grace. However, in this book we try to address distortions of Jesus' message of forgiveness and the reasons why so many people have difficulty with it. Our language is geared to reach the broadest possible audience, including those who have been hurt by traditional religion.

The second way this book differs is that at the time *Healing Life's Hurts* was published, the new insight for us was the connection between emotions and physical health. Thus we wrote about how the five stages of forgiveness could bring emotional and physical healing as well as spiritual healing. Since then, hundreds of journal articles and books on psychosomatic medicine have confirmed the connection between forgiveness and health and have revolutionized the way that medicine is practiced.

This present book emerges from another revolution currently taking place in our world, one that may have even more far-reaching consequences than that of psychosomatic medicine. This revolution provides an answer to the most serious problem facing our society and our world: the problem of violence.

Part I:

THE STAGES OF HEALTHY FORGIVENESS

White Afrikaner soldiers with bulldozers came upon a group of poor black South African women living in a squatters' village. The soldiers told the women they had two minutes to clear out before the bulldozers would level their village. What could the women do? Most of their men were away at work. Should the women get out guns and use violence to protect themselves from the violence of the Afrikaners? Should they acquiesce and passively allow their homes to be destroyed? Here is what the women did. They knew how puritanical white Dutch Reformed Afrikaners are likely to be. The black women stood in front of the bulldozers and took off all their clothes, including their underwear. The soldiers turned and ran. The squatters' community still retains possession of its village.

Chapter 1

GIVE AWAY YOUR UNDERWEAR

This book is about forgiveness. Anyone who has bothered to buy this book probably knows that forgiveness is a critical part of our deep human longing to give and receive love in enduring relationships. Nevertheless, many of us have good reason not to like being told we should forgive. For example, imagine that you are walking home through a deserted neighborhood on a cold, dark night. Laden down with heavy packages, fear grows within you as you hear footsteps approaching from behind. Next thing you know two men lunge at you, knock you to the ground and beat you unconscious.

Several hours later, you regain consciousness. With your frostbitten hand you wipe your bloodied, swollen right cheek. Then you discover that your attackers stopped at nothing, stealing everything but your underwear. As you slowly feel the rest of your face and check your pain-filled body for broken bones, what is your first thought about the brutes who attacked you? Is it, "I love you and forgive you"? Is it, "I wish I had given you not only my coat and my suit but also my underwear"? How about, "I wish I had turned my other cheek so that I would now have two bloodied cheeks instead of just one"?

DOES JESUS WANT US TO GET HIT AGAIN?

Perhaps one of the most unpopular texts in scripture is the classic passage on forgiveness in Matthew 5:38–42:

> You have heard that it was said, "An eye for an eye and a tooth for a tooth." Do not resist an evildoer. But if anyone strikes you on the right cheek, turn the other also; and if anyone wants to sue you and take your coat, give your cloak as well; and if anyone forces you to go one mile, go also the second mile.

In this text, Jesus seems to be saying that forgiveness means letting ourselves be hit on both cheeks rather than one, and not only allowing our coat to be taken from us but even giving away our "chiton" or "cloak," which is our very underwear!

For years, we resented this passage. Obeying it seemed like a surefire way to end up being a passive doormat that anyone could trample on. Many people have shared similar feelings with us. For example, nine-year-old Mark's parents had saved for a long time to buy him his first new bicycle. One evening the new bicycle was stolen. Mark said, "I hate what Jesus says about also giving away your cloak when somebody steals your coat. It sounds like I can't even try to find the guy who stole my bike and get it back."

When we read Matthew 5:38–42 to an audience of five hundred people in Mexico just after the devaluation of the peso, one woman yelled, "I hate that passage. That's exactly how the United States and our own government treat us." Soon all five hundred people were yelling the same thing. A few months ago we read Matthew 5:38–42 to a group of prison inmates. They said, "We hate that passage. It's just how the guards expect us to act when they mistreat us."

We understood how Mark, the Mexicans and the prison inmates felt. All our study of psychology and our experience in counseling told us that it's unhealthy to passively suffer abuse. It seemed that something was wrong with our understanding of Matthew 5:38–42. Recently we found out that Mark, the Mexicans, and the prison inmates were right, thanks

to scripture scholar Dr. Walter Wink. In his award-winning book, *Engaging the Powers*, Walter helped us understand that Jesus' words probably mean the opposite of what we have usually thought. In Matthew 5:38–42 Jesus invites us to a forgiveness that, far from being passive and self-abusive, actively resists evil, maintains our dignity and invites the person who hurt us to recall his or her own dignity. Following is Walter's explanation of this passage.

TURN THE OTHER CHEEK

Let's set aside for a moment the first two sentences and begin with verse 39b, "But if anyone strikes you on the right cheek, turn the other also." Why does Jesus specify the *right* cheek? Imagine that you are a poor slave in ancient Palestine and your master is facing you and about to strike you. He cannot use his left hand, since it was used only for unclean tasks. Therefore, he must use his right hand. He cannot strike you on your right cheek with a fist or with the front of his right hand, since this would require him to twist or contort his arm. Thus, in order to strike you on your right cheek he will have to use the back of his right hand. In Jesus' culture hitting someone with the back of the hand was a gesture that had a very specific meaning. This gesture was used only by those in a position of more power to humiliate those with less power. Masters would backhand slaves, Romans would backhand Jews, husbands would backhand wives and parents would backhand children. The message was, "Remember your place . . . beneath *me!*"

If you do as the passage says and turn your other cheek (your left cheek) and your master must still use his right hand, then he can no longer backhand you. If he hits you again, he will have to use a fist. Hitting another with a fist was a gesture used only between equals. Thus, by turning your other cheek, you have reclaimed your dignity and communicated that you refuse to be humiliated. You have also invited your master to reclaim his true dignity by examining the lie by which he lives, that one human being is better than another. And you have done all this nonviolently, without striking back.

GIVE YOUR UNDERGARMENT TOO

The next part of the passage says, "and if anyone wants to sue you and take your coat, give your cloak as well." The context is a highly exploitive economic system in which the wealthy landowners used high interest rates for loans to force poor people into defaulting and losing their land. For those who had already lost everything, all they had left to give as collateral on loans was their "himation" (translated here as "coat" and meaning one's outer garment).

The scene unfolds in a courtroom and you, a poor person, are being asked to turn over your outer garment. In effect, your creditor is "taking the shirt off your back." Jesus says, "give your 'chiton' as well." "Chiton" is translated here as "cloak," and means your undergarment.* In Jesus' culture, a chiton might be worn by itself in public without embarrassment. However, since nothing was worn underneath it, giving it away would be as if, in our culture, you gave away your underwear. If you gave away your underwear in our culture, or if you gave away your chiton in Jesus' culture, the result

* In this passage from Matthew, it is actually the chiton, rather than the himation, that is demanded. However, in the parallel passage in Luke 6:29–30 the order is reversed so that what is demanded is the himation. The Jewish practice of giving the outer garment as collateral, referred to in Exodus 22:25–27, makes it evident that Luke's order is correct.

would be the same: you would be naked. In Jesus' culture, it was not so scandalous to be naked yourself as it was to look at another person naked. Your creditor must now experience the humiliation he has tried to bring upon you. As Walter Wink says,

> The creditor is revealed to be not a legitimate moneylender but a party to the reduction of an entire social class to landlessness, destitution, and abasement. This unmasking is not simply punitive, therefore; it offers the creditor a chance to see, perhaps for the first time in his life, what his practices cause, and to repent.

Once again you have regained your dignity by taking back your power to choose your own response, all without violence. Moreover, you have offered your oppressor an opportunity for conversion.

GO A SECOND MILE

The passage continues with, "if anyone forces you to go one mile, go also the second mile." In Palestine in the time of Jesus, Roman occupying soldiers could require the local inhabitants to carry their packs. The packs were quite heavy and Roman subjects hated this practice of forced labor. The Romans were shrewd enough to want to avoid riots and so they passed laws limiting the amount of forced labor that could be required. In the case of packs, a Roman soldier could force a local civilian to carry it only one mile. If the soldier demanded more, he himself could be punished.

Imagine, then, that you are a Palestinian local and a Roman soldier grabs you and demands that you carry his pack. You know how far a

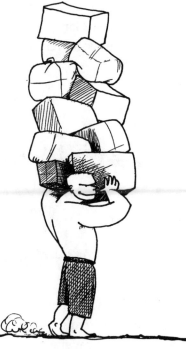

...GO A SECOND MILE...

mile is because the Roman roads were marked. You come to the mile marker, and instead of returning the pack, you cheerfully keep on carrying it. . . . The Roman soldier is now thoroughly confused and afraid he himself will be punished. Imagine him pleading with you to give back his pack! Once again you have regained your dignity by exercising your power to choose your own response and refusing to behave as a victim, all without striking the soldier or otherwise getting caught up in the cycle of violence.

FIND A CREATIVE NONVIOLENT WAY TO RESIST

Let's return then to verse 39a, "Do not resist an evildoer." The word that we translate as "resist" is "antistenai" in Greek. It means to resist *violently,* to rise up in a military sense. Thus, Jesus is telling us not to take an eye for an eye, i.e., not to hit back or otherwise return violence in kind. Instead, when someone tries to abuse or humiliate us, Jesus invites us to find a creative, nonviolent way to resist and regain our dignity. Even in situations of injustice that we cannot fully change, we can at least maintain our power to choose our response instead of being passive victims. As Gandhi said, "The first principle of nonviolent action is that of non-cooperation with everything humiliating."

Forgiveness means we renounce vengeance and retaliation, but it does not mean passive acquiescence to abuse. Walter Wink calls this "Jesus' third way of nonviolent engagement."

Chapter 2

THE TWO HANDS OF FORGIVENESS: FROM PARENTING TO POLITICS

. . . nonviolence gives us two hands upon the oppressor—"one hand taking from him what is not his due, the other slowly calming him as we do this."

Barbara Deming

In Matthew 5:38–42, Jesus teaches us to extend these two hands of nonviolence and forgiveness. The one hand takes from the oppressor what is not his due. This hand says to the oppressor, "No, you can't do that anymore. You cannot humiliate me by backhanding me on my right cheek. You cannot take away my power to respond by hauling me into a court that upholds unjust laws. You cannot make me into a poor helpless victim who carries your pack."

The second hand of forgiveness slowly calms the oppressor. Thus, the second hand invites the master who hits us, the landowner who exploits us and the Roman soldier who uses us to a moment of reflection. We invite our oppressor to the awareness that oppressing others is ultimately futile and degrades oneself as well as one's victims. With this second hand we cannot always offer friendship, since there are situations in which it would not be safe for us to do so. But we *can* always offer our oppressor our wish for his or her highest good.

The two hands of forgiveness are a way to love those who hurt us and ourselves as well. Used rightly, they free us from passivity in the face of abuse, and they offer our oppressor freedom from his or her abusive behavior. Because love is the essence of Jesus' message, love that forgives through nonviolent engagement is at the heart of the gospel. The following stories offer examples of the two hands of forgiveness ranging from childcare to international relations.

WHAT DO I DO WITH THIS KID?

Six-year-old Kyle had agreed with Diane, his mother, that his chore would be to set the table each evening in time for dinner at 6:00. Two evenings in a row the table was not set on time. Each time Diane discussed the situation with Kyle. On the third evening, at 6:15 the table was still not set. Kyle's hungry sister and father impatiently offered to do it so Diane could serve dinner. Diane said, "If you help Kyle by letting him take advantage of us, you won't really be helping him or us." Diane cheerfully asked the whole family to sit down at the table. She brought a pot of spaghetti from the kitchen and plopped a pile of it down on the bare wooden table in front of each person. Then she piled spaghetti sauce on top, and salad dressing on top of that. Maintaining a calm, friendly and nonshaming attitude, Diane finally brought out the frozen yogurt dessert and put some on top of each person's spaghetti. As astonished Kyle had to eat his food without plates or silverware, he experienced the logical consequence of his failure to set the table. From then on, Kyle set the table on time.

PARENTS DECLARE A STRIKE AND SON FINDS A WAY OUT

Bill and Amy did not know what to do with their normally delightful children, eight-year-old Aaron and six-year-old Tony. For several days the boys had refused to help with household chores and were generally uncooperative. Attempts to dialogue with them did not improve the situation. Finally Bill and Amy called a family meeting. In a calm and loving way they said, "You boys seem to be having some trouble contributing to the family. Since you aren't doing your part, we're going on strike. We withdraw all parental services until further notice. The only thing we'll do is drive you to school." (Bill and Amy felt safe in doing this because of their excellent relationship with their children. Also, their high level of self-awareness meant they could monitor their own feelings and avoid vengeful or punitive attitudes.)

The next morning Aaron and Tony packed their own lunches. All they could think of was olives and applesauce. After school, they asked Amy to drive them to the park. In a firm but friendly voice, she refused. At dinnertime Aaron and Tony hungrily explored the refrigerator. They knew how to grate cheese and operate the microwave. However, after two days of nothing but nachos for dinner, the boys were complaining loudly about the strike. Bill and Amy suggested another family meeting. Aaron and Tony said, "You're our parents! You're supposed to take care of us!" Bill and Amy said, "At least we told you we were going on strike. You boys went on strike first and you didn't even tell us about it."

A long discussion followed about the importance of each person's contribution to the family. As the meeting continued, the story behind the children's misbehavior emerged. Bill's mother was dying, and he had not been *his* normally delightful self lately either. It seemed that Aaron and Tony were feeling their father's pain and unconsciously expressing it through misbehavior. Everyone realized that if they had explored the roots of Aaron and Tony's misbehavior earlier, probably no one would have felt a need to go on strike. The whole family agreed to find better ways to share their pain.

Shortly afterward, a group of Aaron's friends decided they wanted to be enemies with another group of boys. They insisted Aaron be on their side against the others and said, "If you're not on our side, we'll hate you." Aaron came home from school obviously distressed. He had learned in his family that enmity with others was futile, and he had also learned not to be passive in the face of conflict. At bedtime he told Bill, "Dad, I don't want to fight with my friends. But I don't want to go along with them and be enemies with the other boys either. I like all the kids." Bill encouraged Aaron as he searched for a way out of the situation.

The next day, Aaron spoke to his friends. In the same calm and loving voice his parents used with him, he said, "I like you and I like the other boys, too. You're all important to me. I'm not going to be against anybody, so I need you to work out your problem with them." At first Aaron's friends were shocked by his refusal to take sides. Then they agreed to resolve their differences with the other boys. All the rest of that year, both groups of boys were friends with each other and with Aaron.

WHAT WOULD YOUR MOTHER SAY?

An elderly woman was accosted by a young man in his mid-twenties. The man, roughly pushing her backward, demanded her money. The woman quickly regained her balance and, pulling herself squarely up to her full height of 5′2″, said in a firm voice devoid of accusation, "Young man, what would your mother feel like if she knew you were doing this?"

The young man was so taken aback that he just stood for a moment in silence. Then in a half-embarrassed voice he replied, "She'd be real hurt, real disappointed, ma'am."

"I know you'd never want that to happen and neither would I," said the woman as she walked by the young man with a smile and a nod.

ROBBER REFUSES MONEY

A man emerging from a bus station met an armed thief waiting outside. The man burst out with spontaneous concern, "It's cold. Why don't you take my jacket?" As the gunman fumbled awkwardly, the man continued in a natural manner, "I was just going for something to eat. Why don't you join me?" He even offered some money, which the gunman refused.

SLUM LANDLORD SENTENCED TO HIS OWN SLUM

A wealthy slum landlord had exploited his tenants for many years by charging them excessive rent for substandard housing. Finally he was arrested for numerous violations of the housing code. The judge sentenced him to live for one month in one of his own rat-infested, smelly rooms with broken pipes and no heat.

$15,000 PRIZE MONEY UNCLAIMED

Animal rights activists offered a $15,000 prize to anyone who would live like a chicken in a wired cage for one week. Four volunteers were selected, three of whom were farmers. A cage was built proportional to one that would typically be used for four chickens. The cage measured 40 × 40 inches and five feet, three inches tall. The only food was cold beans and rice, dispensed every few hours. In imitation of the noise in a hen house, a tape recorder constantly played human screams. The volunteers lasted exactly eighteen hours.

PARISHIONERS' BOYCOTT

A parish in New England had a very progressive pastor who worked cooperatively with the parishioners. The parish community was so healthy and vital that people came from long distances to participate in it. Without consulting the community, the local chancery transferred the pastor and assigned another to take his place.

The new pastor's style was highly authoritarian. For example, on Sunday mornings before Mass he stood at the front door of the church and asked worshipers where they lived. When he discovered people who came from other parishes, he ordered them to go home.

After repeated attempts to dialogue with the new pastor, the community decided it could not work well with him. They feared that all the good they had accomplished with his predecessor would be destroyed. They gathered together and decided to withhold their donations to the parish. The chancery heard what the people were saying and replaced the new pastor with someone more acceptable to the parishioners. The chancery also modified its policy of transferring pastors, to include more consultation with local communities.

JUDGE SENDS CULPRITS TO STUDY HALL

A rabbi discovered that the walls of his synagogue had been defaced with ugly graffiti, including swastikas. He called the police, who found the culprits—a group of local college students. The young men were arrested and charged with vandalism. As the judge was about to sentence them, the rabbi intervened. He said, "I don't want these boys to have a police record, but I do want them to learn respect for my religion. I suggest you release them on condition that they spend thirty hours studying Judaism with me." The judge agreed and the students began regular classes with the rabbi. Their former ignorance was replaced with understanding and respect for the Jewish faith and for the rabbi.

MENORAHS IN EVERY WINDOW

One December evening, the Schnitzer family was preparing their home in Billings, Montana for Chanukah. They taped a yellow plastic menorah to the window of five-year-old Isaac's bedroom. That night the window was suddenly shattered by a cinderblock, thrown by members of a neo-Nazi hate group that had been terrorizing minority groups in Billings for the past year. The next morning the FBI advised Tammie Schnitzer to remove all signs of Chanukah from her home. But Tammie decided that if she backed down in the face of terrorism, neither she nor her family would ever be safe.

The Schnitzers taped the broken window and left the menorahs up. Tammie called *The Billings Gazette* to report what had happened. A day later Marge Mac-Donald, Executive Director of the Montana Association of Churches, read about the attack on the Schnitzers' home. She decided to put a menorah up in her own window, as a sign of solidarity with the Schnitzers. Marge called her pastor and that Sunday he urged the congregation to take home color-in pictures of menorahs, color them in as a family, and hang them in their windows.

The idea spread. The Billings Coalition for Human Rights began running off pictures of menorahs, trying to keep up with the demand from all the people who wanted to support their Jewish neighbors. Dry cleaners and convenience stores gave out paper menorahs provided by the Human Rights Coalition. One store called for more after they went through five hundred copies in one day.

The Billings Gazette published a full-page color menorah and encouraged its 50,000 subscribers to hang it in their windows. The eighth grade students at St. Francis Upper School decorated menorahs and hung them for passersby to see. They were told they could move their desks away from the windows in case of an attack, but they refused. Many churches and Christian homes that displayed menorahs were attacked by the neo-Nazis, but the community refused to back down.

On the eighth and last night of Chanukah, Tammie and Brian Schnitzer drove their children around Billings. Menorahs were everywhere. Isaac said, "I didn't know so many people were Jewish." His mother answered, "They're not all Jewish. But they're our friends." Since then, terrorist attacks against minorities in Billings have stopped. Christian families still display their menorahs at Chanukah each year, in solidarity with the Jewish community.

LATINOS SERENADE KKK

The Hispanic Council of Belsenville, Illinois discovered that the Ku Klux Klan was planning a rally at the county courthouse. They decided to protest the Klan's racism by serenading the KKK with a 13-piece mariachi band. The Council president said, "We'll turn it into a festival where Latino culture is placed high in front of its worst detractors."

FORGIVENESS OVERCOMES AN ARMY

Guatemalan soldiers commonly send spies into local Indian villages to learn about ancient family feuds. They then use this information to divide the people and eliminate indigenous leadership. For example, the spies might learn that the Garcia and Reyes families have been feuding over a land dispute for the past two hundred years. The soldiers would take members of the Garcia family, especially lay catechists or organizers of co-ops, and force them to say that the Reyes family is supporting the guerrillas. They would then take members of the Reyes family and induce them to say something similar about the Garcias. The soldiers would then arrest members of both families and use the false information as an excuse to torture and kill them all.

In one small mountain village the people realized that it was the unhealed hurts between them that made them vulnerable to the government soldiers. They invited us to give a retreat on forgiveness. They then spent the following year uncovering and healing the hurts between families. The next time the soldiers entered the village, all 2,000 people came out into the square and silently stood in a large circle as a sign of their solidarity with one another. With their bodies they communicated to the soldiers, "We are one people, and if you want to take one of us you will have to take us all." The soldiers left and have not returned. This village is now one of the safest in Guatemala.

DANISH PEOPLE SAVE THEIR JEWS

During World War II, when the Nazis informed Denmark's King Christian that they were about to take over his country and that Jews would be required to wear the yellow star, King Christian replied that if the Danish Jews were forced to wear a yellow star, then he, too, would wear one. As a result, the yellow star was never introduced in Denmark. Then the Nazis ordered the Danes to establish a ghetto for the Jews. King Christian refused. He said that if there were such a ghetto, he and his family would move from his palace to be with the Jews.

The Nazis then devised a secret plan to arrest all the Danish Jews on October 1, 1943 (the Jewish New Year). Four cargo ships were waiting to take the Jews to concentration camps in one mass deportation. The Danish government discovered the plan and alerted the Danish people, who went out into the streets and searched for Jews in order to warn them. All over Denmark rescue groups sprang into action. They escorted the Jews to small villages by the sea where they were smuggled across the water into the safety of Sweden.

The solidarity of the Danish people on behalf of the Jews was so great that when money was needed for rescue operations, "you simply went to a bank and asked the teller for 5,000 or 10,000 kroner, stating your purpose, and the money was promptly handed to you." There is no record that anyone ever took advantage of this for personal gain.

Through nonviolent engagement almost all the seven thousand Danish Jews were saved, to the point that Adolf Eichmann admitted that "the action against the Jews of Denmark had been a failure."

NONVIOLENT ENGAGEMENT WORKS

Hitler and the Nazis have often been used as the ultimate excuse for resorting to violence, by those who assume that nonviolence would be impotent against such evil. However, as Walter Wink points out, not only in Denmark but throughout Europe whenever organized nonviolent engagement (vs. passive nonresistance) was tried against the Nazis it *did* work. Unfortunately, it was not often tried.

As we write this more than fifty years later, the prevalence of violence in the news can easily obscure an astonishing movement that is happening all around us. Perhaps most of us can remember November 9, 1989 when the Berlin Wall came down. In that same year, 1,695,100,000 people (32 percent of humanity) in thirteen different countries experienced nonviolent revolutions. If we consider all the countries where major nonviolent actions have taken place in the twentieth century, the total number of people involved is almost three and a half billion, or 64 percent of humanity.

From contemporary parenting classes that replace the violence of punishment with logical consequences (such as Kyle's experience of having to eat a spaghetti/frozen yogurt mess with his fingers), to international politics, humanity is slowly recognizing the power of Jesus' third way of nonviolent engagement, expressed through Barbara Deming's image of the two hands. Outer nonviolence begins with inner nonviolence. The next chapter explores how the five stages of forgiveness provide a process for being with ourselves in a nonviolent way, so that we can be with others in a nonviolent way.

Chapter 3

NONVIOLENT ENGAGEMENT & THE FIVE STAGES OF FORGIVENESS

Several months ago while Sheila and I (Dennis) were traveling from California to Colorado, we experienced forgiveness through nonviolent engagement. Driving into Las Vegas, we saw many signs advertising cheap buffet meals, an enticement casinos offer in hopes you will stop at their establishment to gamble. We're not gamblers, but our food cooler was almost empty. Besides, I love to eat and can't resist a bargain.

We decided to stop at a hotel where the All-You-Can-Eat Buffet was only $3.59. Sheila, who wanted only salad, eyed the expansive salad bar and assured me that I had made a good choice. The hostess asked us to pay in advance, and I gave her $3.59 for each of us. While Sheila loaded her plate with salad, I headed for the healthy food . . . like french fries, ham, deep-fried chicken, and pecan pie. I made several return trips, especially as they kept bringing out new things like pizza and ice cream.

Meanwhile, I noticed that Sheila wasn't eating much. True, she had made three trips back and forth to the salad bar, but only because she was trying to find some-thing edible. It turned out that most of the vegetables were old and rotten. Finally, in desperation she headed for the fruit section only to find out that even the melon balls were slimy. Sheila called for the waiter, and told him about the food. The waiter talked to the manager who eventually came over to our table. Here is how the conversation went:

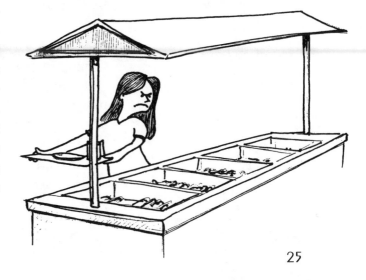

Sheila: All the food I tried was spoiled. I don't think I should pay for
             my meal.
Manager: There's nothing wrong with our food.
Sheila: Look at this melon. It's slimy. Try it for yourself.
Manager: I don't like melon and I'm not giving you your money back!

Then he turned his back on us and walked away. I felt helpless.

FINDING A CREATIVE SOLUTION

Sheila said to me, "If I leave now without doing something about this, I'm going to be really upset with that man and with myself." On the way into Las Vegas we had listened to a tape on assertiveness. The speaker said that when you aren't being treated well as a customer, always talk to the person in charge. So Sheila walked over to the hostess and said, "I want to talk to the owner of this hotel." The hostess said, "He's in Japan." Sheila tried again: "I want to talk to the assistant owner." The speechless hostess went to have a conference with the manager.

Meanwhile, I was growing angrier at the disrespectful way the manager was treating Sheila. I began thinking of how to get even. I imagined bringing in our

food cooler from the car and filling it with about $30 worth of ham, chicken and pizza. (I figured the ice cream wouldn't keep.) But Sheila convinced me that vengefully getting even in this way was no better than the manager's getting even with us for criticizing his food.

Often when I want to vengefully get even, something more is underneath my anger that I am not acknowledging. At such times, I find it helpful to ask myself, "If I were not feeling anger, what would I be feeling?"

I realized that I wanted to become invisible and go away. Then I knew I was feeling shame. I felt shame at allowing myself to be duped. After all, it was I who in good faith had paid the bill before we had gotten any food. Not only did I feel anger over the way the manager was treating us, but I also felt shame for being so gullible. My shame was telling me, "This is all your fault. Why didn't you check out the food more carefully before you paid the bill? All this for $3.59! What's the use of you saying anything to the manager? Let's just get out of here."

When I allowed myself to acknowledge and be with the shame that festered beneath my anger, I no longer wanted to vengefully strike back. As long as I had focused only on how angry I felt at how the manager was treating Sheila, I was doing violence to myself by denying my feelings of shame. And by making myself invisible and wanting to ignore the manager, I was treating him in just as disrespectful a way as I was accusing him of doing to Sheila. I could no longer see myself as an all good victim and the manager as an all bad oppressor. The division between us began to fade. I had become centered in the truth of myself as a good yet fallible person and so I could see the manager in the same way. I now wanted to connect with him in a way that respected both of us.

By then Sheila and I were standing near the entrance to the restaurant. As the customers came in, they asked us, "How's the food?" I thought to myself, "All I have to do is be myself and tell the truth." I told them the pizza and ham were great. But I cautioned them against making the same mistake I had and suggested that they might want to look at the salad bar before they paid their $3.59. I escorted them over to the salad bar and showed them the rotten broccoli and the spoiled carrots, telling the customers, "I'm sure the manager wouldn't want anyone to get sick." Most of them left before I got as far as the moldy sprouts. After about ten

minutes, the waiters started removing the spoiled food from the salad bar. I was left with only slimy melon to show the customers.

At this point, the manager came over, put $3.59 in my hand and said politely, "The assistant owner is Mr. Suzuki. Here's your money back." I thanked him and exchanged a friendly handshake. We left the restaurant, surprised that by simply staying centered in ourselves and telling the truth, we had found a way to resolve the situation without getting even and without letting ourselves be abused.

THE FIVE STAGES OF FORGIVENESS

What does all this have to do with forgiveness? Over twenty-five years ago Dr. Elisabeth Kübler-Ross discovered that her dying patients typically passed through five stages of grief: denial (I'm not really sick), anger (it's the doctors' fault), bargaining (God, I'll stop smoking if you let me live), depression (why didn't I get a checkup sooner?) and acceptance (I really am going to die and I can accept it).

We discovered that, since any hurt is a loss that is like a small death, we pass through these same five stages in forgiving a hurt. Thus, for many years we have written and taught about forgiveness, applying Kübler-Ross' five stages to the process of moving through any hurt: denial (it didn't really bother me), anger (it's their fault), bargaining (I'll forgive if they apologize), depression (it's my fault) and acceptance (I'm not glad for what happened but I'm glad for the gifts that came out of it).

FIVE STAGES

	Stage	In Dying	In Forgiveness
	DENIAL	I don't ever admit I'm dying.	I don't admit I was hurt.
	ANGER	It's their fault that I'm dying.	It's their fault that I'm hurt.
	BARGAINING	I set up conditions to be fulfilled before I'm ready to die.	I set up conditions to be fulfilled before I'm ready to forgive.
	DEPRESSION	It's my fault that I'm dying.	It's my fault that I'm hurt.
	ACCEPTANCE	I look forward to death bringing release from the hurt of dying.	I look forward to growth from the hurt.

Kübler-Ross says that dying persons will automatically move through the five stages of dying if they have a significant other with whom they can share their feelings. We have found that the same is true of the five stages of forgiveness. The five stages of forgiveness, when shared with a significant other, describe our built-in process for healing emotional and spiritual wounds.

Although a physical wound can heal in a sudden and miraculous way, normally we go through a built-in process of physical healing that has discernible stages in which a scab forms and eventually fades away. Similarly, an emotional wound can heal in a sudden and miraculous way in which we are given an immediate free gift of forgiveness. Normally, however, we go through the five-stage process of forgiveness that is as natural to human beings as the formation of a scab over a physical wound.

What do the five stages of forgiveness have to do with Jesus' third way as described by Walter Wink in his exegesis of Matthew 5:38–42? When we first read Walter's book, we were delighted by Jesus' three creative ways of responding to a hurtful situation (turning our cheek, giving away our underwear, and walking the extra mile). Although we could imagine that every hurtful situation has such a creative solution, we wondered how we could ever help release in ourselves and in others the creativity to actually find such solutions. What helped in answering this question was to look back on our own lives and reflect on times when, in hurtful situations, we had acted creatively, as in the example of the Las Vegas salad bar. We realized that creative solutions emerged, often spontaneously, whenever we stayed centered or connected to our true selves. Creative solutions cannot be forced, and when they don't emerge naturally it's generally because we are not centered in ourselves. One of the most helpful ways to get centered is the five stages of forgiveness.

Each of the five stages is like a chapter in a story, revealing a part of ourselves that we are tempted to push away. The human psyche is such that when we deny any part of ourselves, we are no longer at home within and we lose our sense of centeredness as well. When we listen respectfully to all five chapters in the story of a hurt, we regain our center and a creative solution can emerge naturally.

For example, in the story of the Las Vegas salad bar I (Dennis) began by being upset that the manager would not return Sheila's $3.59 and was treating her disrespectfully. As our impasse with the manager continued I was ready to give up, thinking, "All this for $3.59!" The breakthrough came when I stopped my **denial** of the shame that was festering beneath my anger. When I stopped treating myself disrespectfully by listening to what I was denying, I could stop treating the manager disrespectfully and stop blaming him for treating Sheila disrespectfully. At first the focus of my **anger** was the manager's disrespectful treatment of Sheila. Then it was his disrespectful treatment of me. In the **bargaining** stage I went from "I could forgive the manager if he treated Sheila respectfully and gave her back her $3.59" to "I could forgive the manager if he acknowledged me as a person." Finally, in the **depression** stage I began blaming myself for not checking the salad bar more carefully before deciding to eat there. I also realized that in my temptation to say "All this for $3.59! Let's just get out of here," I was being just as impersonal with the manager as I was accusing him of being with Sheila. It was hearing the full story of each stage that eventually led us to the **acceptance** stage and the creative solution of giving would-be customers accurate information before they went through the food line, while at the same time treating the manager with respect.

Thanks to Walter Wink, we realize that Jesus' teaching on nonviolent engagement is also a teaching on creative forgiveness. Most of us know that forgiveness means not striking back, but few of us have learned that ideally it also means nonviolently resisting abuse. Rather than finding Jesus' third way of nonviolent engagement, typically people get stuck in either the anger stage or the depression stage.

If we return violence in kind, taking an eye for an eye, or retaliating by bringing in the food cooler and filling it with $30 worth of ham and pizza, we get stuck in the second stage of anger. Recalling the image of the two hands, we overuse the first hand that says, "You may not take from me what is not your due," and we forget to use the second hand that reaches out to the other. If we passively let ourselves be backhanded again and again on the right cheek, give in to our helplessness as the manager turns his back on us, or remain in a shame attack for not having checked the food more carefully before paying for it, we get stuck in the fourth stage of depression. In terms of the two hands, we forget to use the first hand and overuse the second one.

Why didn't I get stuck? Generally, the more loved I feel the more I can love and forgive others. If I had been alone or had not felt so loved by Sheila, I might have done nothing about the manager and left the restaurant angry or depressed. As we shall see throughout the rest of this book, the more I am loved in the midst of whatever I am feeling the more I can listen carefully to the very things that might otherwise keep me stuck, until they too reveal a creative solution.

Not only the anger and depression stages but each of the five stages helps us explore the whole story of how we have been hurt and find a creative response to the situation without retaliating and without passively suffering abuse. Jesus showed us a third way, a way of forgiveness that not only can preserve our own health and the health of our relationships but also can bring healing to many of our social problems. Whether forgiveness means turning the other cheek, giving away our underwear, walking the extra mile, escorting customers to the salad bar, or something even more surprising, at its best healthy forgiveness involves a creative solution.

In the following chapters, we will share several stories of forgiveness. In the story of John in Chapters 4 through 8, we forgave well enough by most standards but we failed to find a truly creative solution. We will share some of the mistakes we made because we missed some of what the five stages of forgiveness had to offer us. In Chapter 10, "Tomato War," we drew upon the five stages in such a way that we did find a creative solution. We hope the five stages of forgiveness will further unleash that creativity in you.

INTRODUCTION TO
THE FIVE STAGES

WHO IS THE PERSON YOU WOULD LEAST LIKE TO HAVE WITH
YOU IN YOUR BOAT?

Imagine that you are on a Caribbean cruise. Your cruise ship sinks and you paddle a lifeboat to a deserted paradise island. Who is the person you would least like to have with you in your boat? How do you feel when you imagine living with this person on the island?

The person you think of is probably someone with whom you have an unhealed hurt. As you read Chapters 4 through 8, about the five stages of forgiveness, at each stage you may want to be with your feelings toward this person.

Chapter 4

DENIAL

What does the five stage forgiveness process for healing a hurt look like in real life? Following is the story of a hurt that we experienced. The details of this story are based only loosely on the actual events. It is not the details that are most important, but rather the forgiveness process that we are attempting to illustrate. We chose this story because it involves all three of us. Our personalities are quite different and each of us went through the forgiveness process differently. Our hope is that these three different ways of dealing with a hurt will enable most readers to identify with at least one of us.

Several years ago we gave a talk at a Christian conference. The talk was recorded and the tape was later distributed widely throughout the United States by the organization that sponsored the conference. Soon afterward the conference coordinator sent us a copy of an angry, condemning letter he had just received from another author whom we'll call John. We had used one of his stories of healing in our talk, indicating clearly that the story came from him. John said we had misused his story. He demanded that it be removed from the tape.

We felt deeply distressed by the possibility that we had misrepresented John.

So, we reread his magazine article where the story originally appeared. Although it was true that we had recalled a detail incorrectly, it still seemed to us that our overall interpretation of John's story was a reasonable one and that many other readers would have understood it as we did.

However, we were eager to do whatever we could to satisfy John. Matt was worried that he might have made a mistake. Sheila was feeling shame at the possibility that someone might disapprove of her, and thinking she deserved John's harsh criticism. Dennis didn't want any trouble. We all wanted to be "good." So, we wrote John a letter of apology. We assured him that we would ask the distributor of the tape to edit out John's story.

John sent us a note thanking us for our apology and assuring us of his forgiveness. We thought, "That wasn't so bad. It could have been worse. Now let's get back to work." But we found ourselves unable to concentrate. Although we didn't realize it at the time, we had not addressed the real hurt in this situation: we had quoted John because we respected him, yet he had complained to a third party rather than respecting us enough to also come to us. We had asked John to forgive us at a professional level, but had never addressed our need to forgive him for not caring for us at a personal level. This is the stage of denial. Either we pretend that we have not been hurt at all, or we ignore the *real* hurt and focus on less painful aspects of it. Moreover, current hurts may trigger unresolved pain from similar earlier hurts, about which we are still in denial.

When I (Matt) am in denial, what I am most trying to avoid are feelings of anger. I fear anger because, as the shortest child in our neighborhood, I was always beaten in fights. Yet my anger sneaks out and I become negative and critical, noticing crooked pictures and unwashed cups.

When I (Sheila) am in denial, what I am most trying to avoid is shame. I am easily overwhelmed by shame because I was harshly criticized as a child and I have an underlying fear that there is something fundamentally wrong with me. I get very busy at things I can do well, such as cooking.

When I (Dennis) am in denial, what I am most trying to avoid is confrontation. I fear confrontation because several times when I tried it as a child, bigger children put me on top of a water fountain and told me I was all wet. Now, when there's a problem I'm likely to say, "Let's go have fun and deal with this when we come back." Then I make sure we don't come back on time.

Other symptoms of denial may include:

- My breathing is shallow.
- I feel numb and don't take things in (reading and not knowing what I just read).
- I can't enjoy the present moment (not really tasting a strawberry).
- I relapse into my favorite addiction (binging on ice cream after I receive bad news).

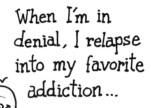

When I'm in denial, I relapse into my favorite addiction...

- I change the subject when others try to express pain.
- I overreact to other people's pain (crying harder than anyone else at a movie).
  - I underreact to other people's pain (I'm the only one in the theater who *isn't* crying).
  - I feel confused and disoriented (driving the wrong way down a one-way street or forgetting where I parked my car).
  - I'm uncomfortable with silence and solitude (leaving the TV on all day).
  - I feel anxious and hyper-vigilant (jumping every time the phone rings).
- I say what I think others want to hear rather than what I really feel (telling someone it's ok to smoke when really cigarette smoke bothers me).
- Life seems flat and meaningless (I can't think of anything I'm grateful for).

I feel anxious and hypervigilant.

What's healthy about denial?

- Keeps me from getting overwhelmed by too much pain at once.
- Allows me to set things aside until I'm in a time and place in which I can deal with them.
- Provides time for me to take in the healing love I need before I can face the hurt.

DENIAL keeps me from getting overwhelmed by too much pain at once.

How denial can affect my health:

Denial can shorten my life when it keeps me from working through emotions that I need to face. For example, metastatic breast cancer kills most women within two years. But forty-three women at Stanford University met once a week in small groups to support each other in processing feelings and hurts they had previously denied. They lived twice as long as another group of forty-three women who were not meeting to share their feelings.

On the other hand denial can keep me from being overwhelmed, even to the point of saving my life. For example, in a group of trapped coal miners only one

man had a watch. The others asked him to call out each passing hour as they waited to be rescued. Since only he knew the real time, he decided to keep up the others' hope by letting two hours pass before calling out one hour. It took a week for the rescuers to reach the coal miners. All but the one with the watch thought it took only three and a half days. Everyone survived except the man with the watch. He could not deny that a week had passed and he gave up struggling for life just before the rescuers arrived.

How I tempt myself when I'm in denial. I minimize the situation by telling myself:

- "It's not so bad."
- "I can handle this."
- "If I ignore this it will go away."
- "I shouldn't bother anyone by getting upset about this."
- "Don't rock the boat."

How others tempt me. They try to distract me by telling me:

- "Don't worry. It will all work out."
- "Time heals all wounds."
- "Forget about it. Let's go shopping."
- "I don't want to talk about that. Let's talk about something pleasant."

How others can help me when I'm in denial:

- Love me just as I am without trying to fix me or change me.
- Listen to what I am feeling and feed back to me what you hear so I know I am understood.
- Help me with simple, practical things that I'm in too much shock to do for myself right now.

Help me with simple, practical things that I'm in too much shock to do for myself right now.

Things I can do to help myself:

- Allow myself to remain in denial for as long as necessary, until I feel loved enough to face the pain of the hurt.
- Put myself in situations where I feel that I belong and can take in the love I need.
- Stay away from people who think they know what I need and what I should do.

HEALING PROCESS TO MOVE THROUGH DENIAL

There are many questions that can help us move through denial. For example, we may ask ourselves, "When the phone rings, whom would I least want on the other end of it?" or, as suggested earlier, "With whom would I least want to be on a desert island?" When I (Matt) am in denial I don't want to admit that I am angry. Since I am a towering five foot three, I have learned over a lifetime to swallow my anger rather than express it to whoever is taller and angry too. I need to go to a safe place where I feel loved by God and others. Then, the question that most helps me to move through denial and get in touch with my anger is, "What am I least grateful for?" I try to do this every evening, as a way of getting in touch with hurts from the day that I may be denying. You may wish to try any of the three questions suggested here, or make up your own question that helps you move through denial.

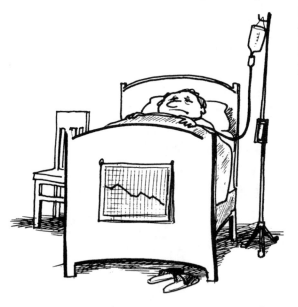

"What am I least grateful for?"

Chapter 5

ANGER

About two weeks after our exchange of letters with John, a friend called and said, "I've been very concerned about you since I received John's letter." We were confused, not knowing why our friend would have received a copy of John's letter to the conference coordinator. But we soon realized that our friend was talking about another letter . . . a very long letter in which John harshly criticized not only our entire tape and its theology but also our personal characters. A few days later we received two copies of John's letter, from two other concerned friends. As we eventually discovered, John had sent his letter to several hundred Christian leaders, including many of our professional colleagues. It seemed that about the only people he *hadn't* sent his letter to had been us.

We noticed that the date of this letter was prior to the date of the letter John had sent the conference coordinator. It was as if he were saying, "I have decided to discredit you regardless of how you respond to my demand that you delete my story." We were also struck by John's earlier note saying he forgave us. If this is how John forgives, we mused as we read his long letter, we prefer not to be forgiven!

At first our denial deepened to a stunned state of shock. We couldn't believe this was happening. Then, finally, we were angry—really angry. We didn't mind John disagreeing with our theology. What angered us was that he had harshly attacked us as persons and had done so in a public letter, without even bothering to send us a copy. We tried to rationalize by telling ourselves that ultimately God's opinion of us mattered more than human opinion. But realistically our ministry depends upon our good reputation, and we were angry at the possibility of having it damaged.

We feared that John's criticism would undermine our credibility and seriously limit our capacity to reach people through our books, tapes and retreats.

The gift of anger is that it locates our wound, helps us defend ourselves and energizes us to correct what needs correction. We wrote to John, asking for a personal meeting to discuss the situation. He never responded. In frustration we went to Paul, a friend of ours and of John's, and asked Paul if he would call John on our behalf. Paul agreed and dialed John's number. John told Paul that it was not his (John's) place to talk with us because he was not a theologian and he thought the theologians needed to work it out. John, who had publicly attacked our theology in detail, was now claiming that he was not a theologian and therefore could not talk with us!

The gift of anger
is that it locates
our wound.

Although we have had no contact with John in the many years since then, we still find ourselves angry at him for refusing to communicate with us. Lingering anger usually indicates we moved too quickly through the forgiveness process. We believe that in an abusive situation we have no right to forgive until we have honored our anger. Anger at abuse and injustice is an expression of our integrity and our dignity as human beings. We must honor our anger before we forgive because authentic forgiveness comes from the same place of integrity deep within us.

One way to honor anger is by listening to it. For example, when John refused to talk with us, there was little we could do since he lived far away and had an unlisted phone number. But when Paul called him in our presence, John's phone number was evident to Sheila as she saw Paul dial it. One of our anger fantasies was to take shifts sleeping so we could call John every fifteen minutes until he agreed to talk with us. We ignored this fantasy, since it seemed mean and vengeful.

But in completely ignoring the fantasy we failed to listen to the gift it might have given us. If we had listened, the fantasy might well have been saying, "Find a way that is not mean or vengeful in which John will be reminded of the harm he has done to you. Find a way to invite him to make amends." Today, several years later, we've thought of some creative ways of doing this that we missed at the time because we didn't listen carefully enough to our anger fantasies. In the anger stage the most common traps are either to act out our anger through vengeful behavior or to bury it and swallow the abuse, rather than listen to what the anger most needs.

We did not bury all our anger. As a way of channeling some of our anger and for our own peace of mind, we sent John's letter along with a copy of our tape to several theologians. They assured us that our theology was sound. Some, on their own initiative, wrote to John and defended us. Slowly our anger diminished as we

saw that others understood our viewpoint and were "enlightened witnesses" on our behalf. An enlightened witness is a person who will listen to us, validate our feelings and experience, protect us from further hurt, and help correct the situation.

When I (Sheila) am angry, I write letters in which I marshal evidence to prove that the person who hurt me is wrong.

When I (Dennis) am angry, I talk down to others in a harsh and scolding voice as if they were ignorant.

When I (Matt) am angry I become extremely impatient. I push elevator buttons every three and a half seconds, continually switch lines at the grocery store checkout and find it difficult to listen without debating.

Other symptoms of anger may include:

- I engage in passive-aggressive behaviors such as:
    being late (for meetings with people I don't like),
    forgetting things (names of people
      I don't like),
    calling in sick when I'm not,
    cutting in front of other
      drivers,
    saying "Yes, but . . . "
- I finish other people's
  sentences.
- I rush through yellow or
  red traffic lights.

- I absolutize ("He always . . . " or "She never . . . ").
- I refuse to participate ("There's no one worth electing so why vote").
- I complain a lot about *other* people's anger and aggression (supporting a multibillion dollar defense budget and harsh, vindictive punishment for criminals).
- I use sarcasm, gossip and negative humor ("He'd be dangerous if he could think").
- I feel distant from God.

What's healthy about anger?

Anger locates our hurt and the depth of it.

- A sign of sensitivity to injustice.
- Locates our hurt and the depth of it.
- St. Thomas Aquinas said that virtue consists in being angry at the right person for the right reasons and for the right amount of time.
- Indicates that the hurt has surfaced and is ready to be healed.
- Energizes us to correct what needs correction.
- Helps us protect ourselves.
- Focuses our power, passion and dignity.

Anger energizes us to correct what needs correction.

How anger can affect my health:

Anger can get stuck inside me and cause heart disease. For example, medical students at Duke University were asked, "How would you feel if someone ahead of you at a ten-item express check-out line had eleven items?" Their responses ranged from denying the hurt to angrily wanting to get even. The medical students with the highest hostility scores (those who were stuck in anger) were seven times more likely to die by age fifty. Their hostility scores were a better predictor of death from cardiac illness than smoking, high blood pressure or a high cholesterol level.

On the other hand, when I befriend my anger and use it creatively, it can save my life. For example, Dr. Bernie Siegel's "exceptional cancer patients" with the longest survival rates are also the angriest patients. This is because they have worked through their anger at whatever hurts and losses they experienced (especially during the year or two

When I befriend my anger and use it creatively, it can save my life.

before the cancer struck). Now they are redirecting that anger to conquer their cancer. Their anger toward cancer comes from their deep love of life. When they are asked, "Do you want to live to be one hundred?" exceptional cancer patients enthusiastically answer, "Yes."

How I tempt myself when I'm angry:

- I try to minimize my anger by telling myself:
   "It could be worse."
   "I should get over this."
   "Nice girls don't get angry."

"Nice girls don't get angry."

"I'm being a spoiled brat just wanting my own way."

"Christians should forgive. If I don't, I'm putting another nail in Jesus' hands."

"It's not worth letting them know how I feel because they'll never change."

- I maximize or act out my anger by telling myself:

  "Don't get mad, get even."

  "If I don't kill him first, he'll kill me."

  "Spare the rod and spoil the child."

  "He deserves to feel the way I feel."

  "You can't trust anyone."

  "If I forgive I'll be vulnerable again."

"If I don't kill him first, he'll kill me."

How others tempt me:

!! SMILE !!

- Deny my anger or encourage me to be passive:

  "You better watch out, you better not pout, Santa Claus is coming to town."

  "Anger is a sin."

  "Do unto others as you would have them do unto you."

  "If you think you have it bad, let me tell you what happened to me."

  Trying to distract me by taking me shopping, buying me toys, feeding me, changing the subject.

- Encourage me to be vengeful:

  "An eye for an eye and a tooth for a tooth."

  "You should sue him." (lawyers' billboards)

  "The only way she'll learn is if you show her who's boss and teach her a lesson."

  "You should sue him."

  "We have to bring him to justice and make him pay for his crime." (capital punishment rather than making amends)

How others can help me when I'm angry:

- Love me just as I am without trying to fix me or change me.
- Listen to what I am feeling and feed it back to me so that I know I am understood.
- Help me identify what it is that I'm really angry about and what I can do to change the situation.
- Ask me if I've ever felt this way before and what helped me.
- If I am unable to restrain myself from acting out my anger in destructive ways, provide boundaries to protect me and others from harm.
- If it's appropriate, speak up on my behalf and intervene to protect me from further abuse.

Things I can do to help myself:

- Physical exercise (dig in the garden).
- Ask my body how it wants to express my anger, and find a way to do this that is not harmful to myself or others (if I feel intruded upon and want to throw someone out of my life, find stones and throw them as hard as I can).
- Write a letter to the person who hurt me (and decide later whether to send it).
- Share with an understanding, loving friend.
- Ask myself if I have ever felt this way before, and let myself be loved with the anger I might still be carrying from a past hurt that is being triggered by the present hurt.
- Confront the other person without blaming ("When you did X, I felt Y, and I need Z").
- Sometimes the one we need to confront is God. Give myself permission to be angry at God, and share it with God and others.

- Join a support group, such as Adult Children of Alcoholics.
- Join an activist group that is working to correct the problem, such as MADD (if my child was killed by a drunk driver), The Link-Up (if I was sexually abused by a clergyperson) or Amnesty International (if I was tortured).
- Hang around people who have what I lost and need to recover (if my father couldn't love me, find a healthy fatherly person who can give me appropriate fatherly love).
- If I feel overwhelmed by anger (or any other feelings) get professional help.

HEALING PROCESS TO MOVE THROUGH ANGER

1. Imagine yourself in the presence of someone who loves you, such as God, your best friend, etc.

2. Get in touch with the hurt you've experienced and your feelings of anger.

3. Share with God or your best friend your feelings about the hurt, expressing all your anger. Include what you lost and what you need. You may wish to do this in the form of a letter. If so, write your letter in the present tense, as if the hurt were happening to you right now.

4. Listen for how God or your best friend would respond. If you've written a letter, let God or your best friend write back to you.

5. Breathe in the ways God or your best friend wants to love you.

Chapter 6

BARGAINING

Bargains ("I'll forgive you if . . . ") ask for changes we want in the other person before we will be willing to move further through the forgiveness process. An easy way to discover our bargains is to write out the ideal apology letter we would want to receive from that person. For example, our dream letter from John went like this:

> I'm sorry that when I had a problem with you I didn't contact you first. If I had, I would have learned that my theological attacks were unjustified. Even worse, my attacks on your character were totally unwarranted. Enclosed is my letter of apology that I will send out to the several hundred people who received my other letter. Please add any corrections or suggestions that you think necessary. If anything like this ever happens again I will communicate directly with you, and you can do the same with me.

In this ideal apology, we expressed two needs. First, that John communicate directly with us, and second, that he write a public apology. Needs are not necessarily bargains. They become bargains only when their fulfillment becomes a precondition for extending our forgiveness. In our case, our two needs were also our two bargains since we were thinking to ourselves, "We will forgive you, John, only if you communicate directly with us, and only if you write a public apology."

Bargains help me discover my
ideal fantasy of what I still need
before I can forgive.

Bargains are healthy because they give voice to our anger by pinpointing not only what we are still upset about but also what we need in order to start the healing process.

Our first bargain pinpointed our need for assurance that if John ever had another problem with us he would contact us first. We hoped this would prevent future misunderstandings from mushrooming into big explosions. Our second bargain was that we needed John to restore any damage done to our reputation by writing a public letter of apology. We needed this because we feared our retreat ministry might be damaged if several hundred Christian leaders believed his criticisms of us. Would we continue to receive retreat invitations? Two of our speaking engagements had already been canceled because of John's letter. Would others be canceled, too?

Even if the person who hurt us cannot or will not respond as we wish, our bargains reveal how we need healing and we can open ourselves to receive this healing in other ways. For example, we wanted John to write a public letter of apology because we were worried about our reputation and we needed reassurance about the future of our ministry. The mail soon did that for us. Not only did we receive affirming letters from theologians, as we mentioned earlier, but other concerned people who had seen John's letter wrote to us also. These people expressed confidence in us and support for our ministry.

At this point it seemed to us that we had a choice: to keep demanding that all would be well only when John changed and apologized, or to take in life from others who could truly heal us. When we can't move on in the forgiveness process until the person who hurt us first changes, we make our happiness dependent on that person and remain a victim. He or she is often very hurt too, and perhaps not free enough to change.

When we look back many years later on this situation, we are glad that we forgave John as best we could, even though he did not change as we wished. However, we also see that our forgiveness was incomplete because we failed to find Jesus' "third way" described by Walter Wink. We let John hit us twice on the right cheek and humiliate us, first by attacking us in a letter to the conference coordinator and then by attacking us even more harshly in a letter to several hundred Christian leaders. We never found a way to turn our left cheek and reclaim our dignity. The challenge in forgiveness is to refrain from vengeance, but at the same time to turn our left cheek, i.e., to do everything in our power to protect ourselves from further abuse.

Each of the five stages is like a chapter in a story. The entire story is about what happened to us, what we need now and how to get it. Hearing the entire story releases our creativity to find a creative third way, a way of turning our left cheek. For example, what if after we possessed John's unlisted phone number we had not buried but rather paid attention to our anger fantasy of calling him every fifteen minutes? We might have heard our fantasy's message: "Find a creative way in which John will be reminded of the harm he has done to you."

One creative way might have been to hold on to the following *bargain:* "John, we will delete your story from our tape only if you give us your mailing list so that we can communicate our side of the situation to the same several hundred people." We believed we could meet our moral obligation to John by correcting the erroneous detail on the tape and editing in the words, "Our interpretation of this story is. . . . "

The ongoing presence of his story on our tape would have reminded John that if he wanted us to go further in caring for his reputation, then he would have to show some care for ours. We didn't think of this at the time because we didn't listen carefully to what the bargaining stage (or the other four stages of forgiveness) had to say to us. Thus, our "forgiveness" became an occasion for allowing John to treat us like a doormat. Forgiveness does not mean tolerating abuse from the person who hurt us, but rather finding a healthy way to love ourselves and that person as well.

Forgiveness does require us to release the other person whether they meet our bargains or not. Otherwise, we will remain tied to that person. But forgiveness also requires us to continue to do everything we can to get our bargains met. Sometimes, as with John, one of our bargains is itself the creative solution that enables us to follow Jesus' third way of nonviolent engagement.

Another way to conceive of bargains is to think of them as boundaries. Boundaries are ways in which we protect our dignity by setting limits on how other people may deal with us. We do others a favor when we clearly communicate to them our boundaries. One of our boundaries is that we are not willing to be mistreated. As we later learned, John had a pattern of treating others in the way he had treated us. We heard of several other situations in which he publicly attacked another person in ministry without first approaching that person directly, and then refused to dialogue about the situation. When we gave up our bargains so quickly, we failed to invite John to deal with the consequences of his behavior and increased the likelihood that he would do the same thing to someone else in the future. Because his letter was so extreme, it ultimately seems to have hurt his reputation more than

"Boundaries are ways in which we protect our dignity by setting limits on how other people may deal with us."

ours. John discredited himself with many people through his unjust treatment of us. We failed him as well as ourselves because we didn't honor our bargains enough to ask that he respect our boundaries and make amends to us. In Barbara Deming's terms, we underused the first hand that says, "No, you cannot treat me this way," and we overused the second hand that reaches out to calm the other.

When I (Dennis) am bargaining, I will forgive the person who hurt me if he or she apologizes and does something to repair the damage.

When I (Matt) am bargaining, I will forgive the person who hurt me if he or she admits that I am right.

When I (Sheila) am bargaining, I will forgive the person who hurt me if he or she listens empathically to me and understands how I feel.

Other symptoms of bargaining include "I'll forgive you if . . . ":

- you change your behavior (arrive on time, lose weight, stop smoking, work harder, etc.),
- you get punished (pay with your life through capital punishment),
- you suffer enough and learn your lesson,
- you feel what I feel,
- you recognize the destruction you did,
- you make amends,
- you promise to never do it again.

I will forgive you IF you make amends.

What's healthy about bargaining?

- Bargains give voice to my anger by pinpointing what I am still upset about and what I need in order to start the healing process.
- They express my boundaries, which protect my dignity by setting limits on how other people may deal with me.
- They invite the oppressor to deal with the consequences of his or her behavior.
- They are often the creative solution that expresses Jesus' third way of non-violent engagement.

How bargaining can affect my health:

When I am not in touch with my bargains and the way they help me set boundaries and express needs, I can exhaust myself by caring for others. For example, Dr. George Solomon found that AIDS patients can ask themselves a simple question to gauge their chances of long-term survival: "Would I do a favor *I really didn't want to do* for a friend who asked me?" Those who say, "No," and refuse to codependently care for others at their own expense are the long term survivors of AIDS.

On the other hand, when I can work through my bargains (I will love you only if) so that I honestly want to offer unconditional love, my immune system is

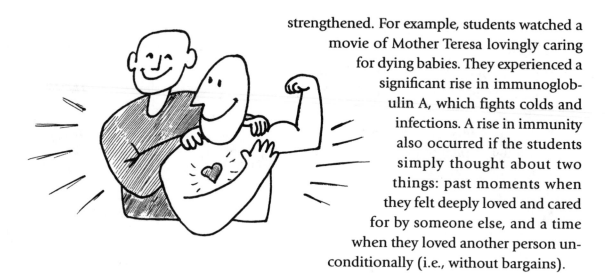

strengthened. For example, students watched a movie of Mother Teresa lovingly caring for dying babies. They experienced a significant rise in immunoglobulin A, which fights colds and infections. A rise in immunity also occurred if the students simply thought about two things: past moments when they felt deeply loved and cared for by someone else, and a time when they loved another person unconditionally (i.e., without bargains).

How I tempt myself when I'm bargaining:

- I dismiss the needs expressed by my bargains and tell myself I shouldn't be so needy.
- I make bargains that are weak and fail to hold the person who hurt me accountable for violating my boundaries.
- I assume there is no way I can get my bargains met, and so I fail to listen carefully to their creative potential.
- I tell myself that if my bargains are not met by the person who hurt me, I will never recover from this hurt.

"I tell myself that if my bargains are not met by the person who hurt me, I will never recover from this hurt."

How others tempt me. They say:

- "Good Christians forgive unconditionally."
- "It's codependent to be needy."
- "The person who hurt you isn't capable of taking responsibility or making amends, so don't even try."
- "The person who hurt you deserves to pay for this. Don't let them off the hook."

"The person who hurt you deserves to pay for this. Don't let them off the hook."

How others can help me when I'm bargaining:

- Love me just as I am without trying to fix me or change me.
- Listen to what I am feeling and feed it back to me so that I know I am understood.
- Help me discover the needs contained in my bargains and find ways to get those needs met.
- Affirm my right to healthy boundaries.
- No matter how outrageous my bargains might seem at first, dream with me of how they may be pointing to a creative solution.

"Affirm my right to healthy boundaries."

Things I can do to help myself:

Listen carefully to my bargains,
assuming they have something
wonderful to teach me.

- Listen carefully to my bargains, assuming they have something wonderful to teach me.
- Hang around people who are in touch with their needs and who have healthy boundaries.
- Ask appropriate people to meet the needs indicated by my bargains, so that I am not dependent on whether or not the person who hurt me responds.
- Attend meetings of Codependents Anonymous, where members are encouraged to establish healthy boundaries.
- If I feel ready to let go of my bargains and move on in the forgiveness process, recall a time when I hurt someone else and that person gave me new life by forgiving me.

HEALING PROCESS TO MOVE THROUGH BARGAINING

1. Imagine yourself in the presence of someone who loves you, such as God, or your best friend.

2. Get in touch with a hurt and share all your feelings about the hurt with the one who loves you.

3. Write out the ideal letter of apology that you would want to receive from the person who hurt you.

4. Identify the one or two main needs contained in your letter.

5. Ask yourself how the person who hurt you or someone else could help you get what you need.

6. Take some deep breaths and fill yourself with life as you imagine yourself saying and doing whatever is necessary to get your needs met.

Chapter 7

DEPRESSION

Once we surface our bargains and begin meeting the needs they reveal, we often move on to the depression stage. Now, instead of blaming the other person (as we did in the anger stage), we blame ourselves. We ask, "What could I have done better before, during or after the hurt?" The value of the depression stage is that it can help us acknowledge our mistakes and discover our power to make changes and amends if needed. This is healthy guilt.

The danger in this stage is that instead of healthy guilt (I made a mistake) we may feel false guilt, in which we blame ourselves for mistakes that are not our fault. The extreme of this is when we take so much blame that we experience toxic shame (I *am* a mistake and I don't deserve to be treated any better). When we feel false guilt or toxic shame we can easily get stuck in depression because our shame makes us feel unworthy of the very thing we most need: love and forgiveness.

When we entered the depression stage, we asked ourselves, "Is there any truth to what John says? Did we make any mistakes for which we need to make amends?" We came up with two things. First, we had recalled a detail of John's story incorrectly. We were traveling at the time we prepared our talk and we did not have John's article (in which the story originally appeared) with us. Since all three of us thought we remembered the story correctly, we didn't check it in the article when we returned home. Now we felt sorry for our carelessness. This was healthy guilt and it motivated us to want to make amends and ask John's forgiveness. Regardless of how John treated us, the three of us were in agreement that even if we kept his story we would make amends by correcting this detail on the tape. The key to health in the depression stage is to honestly admit our mistakes and at the same time take in love and forgiveness, as we did from the many people who wrote and supported us.

Secondly, we blamed ourselves for misinterpreting John's story. The three of us are all extremely conscientious and eager to be "good." We tend to blame ourselves for things that are not our responsibility. Looking back, we see that John wrote his story in such a way that our interpretation was probably the most likely one. Instead of apologizing to him for our interpretation, we wish we had told him that his writing was unclear. We could have advised him to either clarify his story or delete it from *his article.* At the time, however, we took responsibility for the whole situation. Instead of healthy guilt, we were experiencing false guilt.

For us, the trap when we've been hurt is not usually vengeful retaliation (getting stuck in anger). Rather, our trap is swallowing our anger and passively taking abuse, including the abuse we heap upon ourselves (getting stuck in depression). In other words, we tend to underuse the first hand of forgiveness that protects us, and we tend to overuse the second hand that reaches out to the other.

The trap when we've been hurt is not usually vengeful retaliation, but rather passively taking abuse.

With John, we got stuck in depression and this kept us from finding a creative third way. The depression stage gets healed to the extent we can receive love as we take responsibility for our mistakes . . . and do not take responsibility for the mistakes of others.

When I (Matt) am in depression,
I see the glass as half empty rather
than half full. I think of everything
that can go wrong. (When I'm
not depressed, I still think
of everything that can go
wrong but I don't really
believe it.)

When I (Sheila)
am in depression, I
spend the whole day
cooking. (I do that when
I'm not depressed too, but
I don't use as many dishes.)

When I (Dennis) am in
depression, I get cranky and
I complain about all the
dishes Sheila uses when
she cooks.

Other symptoms of depression may include:

- I sleep less or I sleep more. Either way, I feel more tired.
- I don't breathe deeply.
- Either the pepperoni pizza stops looking good, or I can't stop until I've eaten the whole thing.
- I don't want to wear bright colors.
- I keep looking at my clock, hoping it will be later than it is.

I keep looking at my clock, hoping it will be later than it is.

- I don't like what I see in the mirror.
- I find it hard to dream or try new things.
    - I feel helpless because it seems as though anything I think of to change the situation will only make things worse. Why did I ever get myself into this?
        - I am overly sensitive to criticism and long for others to affirm me.

I am overly sensitive to criticism and long for others to affirm me.

- I feel like saying "No" to every request, yet I can't stand up to others and say "No" when they ask me to do something I don't want to do.
- I bend over backward to be nice or to do things for the person who hurt me—things that either I or they don't really want.
- I don't want the phone to ring . . . just leave me alone. Or, I feel clingy and can't stand to be alone.
- I think that whatever I want is probably illegal, immoral or fattening.
- If the world were coming to an end, I believe this would be a good day for it to happen.

I think that if the world were coming to an end, this would be a good day for it to happen.

What's healthy about depression:

- It helps me admit real guilt, forgive myself and make amends.
- It gives me an opportunity to face and change the things I can change rather than be a victim waiting for the other to change.
- It helps me see the ways in which I share humanity with the person who hurt me, so that I no longer divide people into oppressors and victims.

How depression can affect my health:

If I get stuck in the depression stage and feel overwhelmed by feelings of inadequacy and hopelessness, I am more likely to die suddenly, especially of a heart attack. I may well die, as do 75 percent of all those who die at work and 50 percent

of those who die at home, on Monday, especially Monday morning. Monday morning is when we feel most depressed and overwhelmed as we realize all that we have to deal with during the coming week. Those who are prone to recurring heart attacks tend to experience that Monday morning depressed feeling all week long. They often live with "a harsh condemnation of the self, a feeling that you never do anything right, fast enough or good enough." However, those who participated in a group at Stanford University where they could share their feelings had 44 percent fewer recurring heart attacks.

Awareness of our mistakes can also contribute positively to our health. Survivors of near death experiences (NDEs) often report that in the presence of an unconditionally loving, nonjudgmental "Being of Light," they reviewed every moment of their lives at once, including their mistakes. Dr. Raymond Moody, the founder of near death studies, explains that this "life review" is more than watching one's life pass by as if watching a movie screen. The NDE survivor not only "sees" his or her life pass by, but also *experiences* the impact he or she had on all the other people involved. Thus, a woman having an NDE feels the happiness of those people whom she treated lovingly during her life, and she feels the pain of those she treated unlovingly.

For example, a minister who liked to give harsh sermons about hell and damnation had an NDE in which he felt the fear of a nine-year-old boy listening in the congregation. The minister resolved to learn from his mistakes, and when he returned from his NDE he never again preached condemning sermons. Similarly,

Moody reports the cases of two sociopaths (people who behave as if they had no conscience) who had NDEs. They felt all the pain they had caused others, and when they returned, both became extremely loving people. The depression stage can bring healing if, like those undergoing an NDE, we take in love as we face our mistakes.

How I tempt myself when I'm in depression. I tell myself:

- Things will only get worse.
- I should have . . . and should now . . . and should tomorrow. . . .
- There's nothing I can do about it.
- I'll never . . . (get over this) and I'll always . . . (be miserable).
- It's too late. . . .
- It was all my fault. I have to try harder so I won't make a mistake like this ever again.
- If people really knew me, they wouldn't like me.
- No one understands me.
- This is taking too long to heal. When will the pain ever go away?

How others tempt me. They say:

- "You shouldn't feel that way. Cheer up."
- "You have to forgive yourself because Jesus died on the cross for you."
- "Go ahead and sulk if you want to."
- "You brought this all on yourself."
- "You haven't done anything wrong. It was all his/her fault."

"You shouldn't feel that way. Cheer up."

How others can help me when I'm in depression:

- Love me just as I am, especially when I can't stand myself, without trying to fix me or change me. If I have made mistakes, make it obvious that you forgive me.
- Listen to what I am feeling, and feed back to me what you hear so I know I am understood.

Listen to what I am feeling, and feed back to me what you hear so I know I am understood.

- After I know I am loved and understood, ask me if I have ever felt this way before and what helped me then.
- Let me know that you, too, have made mistakes.

Don't categorize me as only a helpless victim.

- Don't categorize me as only a helpless victim or the person who hurt me as only an oppressor. Support me as I discover at my own pace our common humanity.
- Support me in accepting the things I cannot change and changing the things I can.
- If it is appropriate, speak up on my behalf and intervene to protect me from further abuse.
- If I'm so depressed that I can't function in daily life, provide practical assistance. If there's any danger that I will harm myself or another, help me get professional help.

If I'm so depressed that I can't function in daily life, provide practical assistance.

Things I can do to help myself:

- Get physical exercise (walk every day).
- Eat nourishing food.
- Listen to calming music, especially classical music.
- Spend as much time as possible outdoors in beautiful surroundings and work in the garden if I can.
- When I have to be indoors, stay near windows that look out on natural settings.
- Fill my home with plants, and get a pet if possible.

Fill my home with plants, and
get a pet if possible.

- At the end of each day ask myself, "What gave me the most life today?" and do more of it.
- Make a list of the people who love me and stay in touch with them as often as possible.
- Attend a support group meeting.
- Pray in whatever way most helps me to take in God's love.

HEALING PROCESS TO MOVE THROUGH DEPRESSION

1. Imagine yourself in the presence of someone who loves you, such as God or your best friend.

2. Get in touch with a hurt.

3. Ask yourself, "What am I not so grateful for that I did in this situation?" or, "What could I have done differently before, during or after the hurtful situation?"

4. Share your answer with God or your best friend, and let God or that person love and forgive you. Breathe deeply and let love and forgiveness fill your whole body until you can forgive yourself.

5. If necessary, make amends to anyone you have hurt.

Chapter 8

ACCEPTANCE

As we let God and others help us forgive ourselves and make amends for our mistakes, we move out of the depression stage and enter the final stage of acceptance. In acceptance we are grateful for the new life that has come from the hurt. We are not grateful for the destruction we have experienced, but now this seems less than the new growth in giving and receiving life with God, others, the universe and ourselves.

Even though many years have passed, we are still not fully in the acceptance stage with John. Because we did not go through the stages in a healthy way several years ago, we each still have ways that we need to complete them today. Several years ago Dennis got stuck because of his tendency to want to make peace at any price. Sheila got stuck because she thought she deserved the disrespectful treatment we received from John. Matt got stuck because John's angry lashing out at us reminded him of his own capacity to angrily lash out at others.

Thus, today before we will be able to totally forgive John, we will each need to let God and others help us forgive ourselves more deeply in the places where we got stuck. To the extent that we offer ourselves the unconditional forgiveness God is always offering us, we can offer that same unconditional forgiveness to John and to others. Dennis will need to forgive himself for making peace at any price. Sheila will need to forgive herself for thinking she deserves disrespectful treatment.

And Matt will need to forgive himself for not being at home with his anger. Each of us got stuck in our own way according to how we still carried unresolved hurts from earlier life. We can identify these hurts by asking, "When have I felt this way before?" Then we can go through the five stages to heal these earlier hurts.

As we do this, we move more fully into the acceptance stage with John. To the extent we are already there, we can see that our hurt with John brought us new life in several ways. First, we never again wanted to make a mistake in using other people's stories. Now we send our material to the person whose story we are using, to be sure we have quoted him or her correctly.

Secondly, no matter how many theological arguments our friends presented to John on our behalf, he still disapproved of the position we had taken in our talk. We learned from this that we cannot please everyone. This taught us to define our audience more carefully in future talks and books.

Thirdly, through this and other experiences, we've learned the difference between honest theological disagreement and shaming behavior disguised as theology. Now when we receive a disrespectful letter criticizing our theology, we know from the tone of such letters that they are more about shame than about theology itself (see Chapter 13: Focusing Prayer). Instead of wasting our time churning out pages of theological defense, as we did in the situation with John, we simply write back a brief note saying: "Please rewrite your letter in a way that focuses on the issues and avoids personal attack. Then we will be happy to discuss your theological concerns."

Fourth, because we survived John and are learning better ways to handle criticism, we have more courage in speaking and writing about controversial topics. The talk John criticized was our early effort at what eventually became the theme of our most stretching book, *Good Goats: Healing Our Image of God.* In dialoguing with all the people who became involved in the situation with John, we became more confident that our position was valid. In researching the questions John raised we ended up with more than enough material for an entire book, *Good Goats.*

When we first tried to think of the gifts that have come from our hurt with John we could only think of two. Our list is now up to the four we've just mentioned. Like the stage of acceptance, the whole of forgiveness is an ongoing process. As we forgive ourselves more deeply and heal earlier hurts triggered by this one, we will discover more gifts. And, as we discover more gifts, our acceptance will deepen and so will our forgiveness. Thus to the degree we can be grateful for the new life coming from the hurt, we are healed.

When I (Dennis) am in acceptance, I am grateful for even small chores, like washing the dishes.

When I (Matt) am in acceptance, I see the glass as half full rather than half empty.

When I (Sheila) am in acceptance, I feel connected to all of creation.

Other symptoms of acceptance may include:

- I feel at peace with the person who hurt me, whether or not we mutually agree to continue the relationship.
- I feel grateful, not for the hurt itself and the destruction it caused, but for the new life I can see coming from the hurt.
- I wake up rested and eager to start the day, even if I am planning a picnic in a downpour. I feel energized and able to dream.

- I have courage to risk new situations in which I could be hurt again, because I know that healing is possible.
- I want to say "Yes" to reasonable requests, but when someone asks me to do something I don't want to do, I feel free to say "No."
- I can more readily love myself with whatever I am feeling and forgive myself when I make mistakes.
- Colors are brighter, food tastes better, music is more beautiful . . . I enjoy each moment rather than hurrying to finish.
- I am able to give and receive love with other people. When I receive a compliment, I am more likely to say "Thank you" and less likely to say "But . . . "
- I have a sense of belonging to myself, others, God and the universe. I feel wonder and reverence for all of life.

How acceptance can affect my health:

The more I give and receive love and acceptance with others, the more I receive life. For example, those who have the fewest colds are people on their honeymoon. Even though their physical closeness would make it more likely that if one has a cold the other will catch it, the flow of love and acceptance between the new spouses strengthens their immune systems as every cell reaches out for life. Also, we've read that husbands who kiss their wives before going to work suffer less from problems of circulation, digestion, liver and insomnia. They are in far fewer traffic accidents and will live an extra five years. Their wives tend to weigh less, perhaps because a kiss exercises twenty-nine facial muscles (for fewer wrinkles!) and expends twelve calories. Although we can't prove any of this scientifically, we expect that wives who kiss their husbands before going to work gain the same benefits for themselves and their husbands . . .

How I tempt myself when I am in acceptance. I tell myself:

- This is too good to last so I'd better not enjoy it too much and then be disappointed when it's over.
- If some pain from a related loss surfaces, I catastrophize, "Nothing was really healed. I should be able to forgive once and for all."
- Now everything in my life is healed. (This prevents other layers of hurt from surfacing.)

How others tempt me:

- They tell me I'm in denial.
- They "realistically" find something that can go wrong and tell me about it. They say, "But have you thought about . . . ?"

"But . . . have you thought about . . . ?"

How others can help me when I am in acceptance:

- Love me just as I am, and rejoice with me.
- Listen to what I am feeling, and feed back to me what you hear so I know I am understood.
- Affirm me in using my gifts. Healing deepens as I use my gifts to give and receive life with others, God and the universe.

Things I can do to help myself:

- Allow myself to enjoy and fully feel in a bodily way my gratitude.
- Risk using my gifts to foster life and nonviolence.

"Risk using my gifts to foster life and nonviolence."

PROCESS FOR DEEPENING ACCEPTANCE

1. Imagine yourself in the presence of someone who loves you, such as God or your best friend.

2. Get in touch with a hurt that doesn't bother you as much as it used to.

3. In the presence of that person, ask yourself if you can find any gifts that have come out of the hurt. Although you need not be grateful for the hurt and destruction itself, is there any way you are grateful for new life coming from this hurt? Especially, consider how the hurt has helped you belong to yourself, others, God and the universe.

For example, perhaps you were spanked or beaten as a child and your experience motivated you to find nonviolent ways to raise your own children and relate to others. Or, perhaps you were not listened to and as a result you have developed the skill of listening compassionately.

4. Give thanks for the gifts you are aware of and for those you have yet to discover. Ask yourself if there is a way you want to risk using your new gift.

Chapter 9

YOU DON'T HAVE TO FIGURE EVERYTHING OUT

After reading the previous pages, you may be thinking that the five stages of forgiveness sound very complicated. If you are in touch with a hurt, perhaps you don't know how to figure out what stage you are in or how to move from one stage to another. Actually, the stages are not about figuring anything out. Rather, they are about letting yourself be loved wherever you are, with all your thoughts and feelings regarding the hurtful situation. When you do that, you will automatically move from one stage to the next. As the following story exemplifies, you don't have to figure out what stage you are in or plot strategies of how to move from one stage to another.

While the three of us were writing this book, we (Dennis and Sheila) witnessed the slow death of our computer. At first it would freeze once or twice a week. We would then lose whatever we had just written. This was hard on our creativity, but bearable. A trip or two to the computer store had convinced us that it would be easier to put up with what we had. Even computers on sale cost a lot, but most of all we didn't want to take time now to learn all the complexities of the new ones.

Our computer was a thirteen-year-old no-frills model. We know little more about computer technology than how to turn the machine on and off. Yet our no-frills computer, in the last five years alone, had churned out five books. We hoped it would hold out until the end of this book. Unfortunately, when we were within a month of finishing, our computer began freezing not once or twice a week, but once or twice a day. We knew we had to do something.

Shortly afterward, we called a friend in California who loves computers. He said he had a toll-free phone number for an organization that sells discontinued demonstrator models at a low price. We tried the number and got an automated answering service that kept us pushing buttons until it finally asked for our zip code. Then an electronic voice gave us a local phone number, which turned out to be a computer store in the town next to ours.

Jeff answered the phone. He had the exact model we wanted at a price we could afford. We told him we were computer illiterate and that our only hesitation was finding someone who would be available to help us learn to use the new computer. He asked where we lived. We told him our home address. Jeff exclaimed, "I rent the basement room in the house across the street from you! I'll teach you everything you need to know." We made an appointment to see Jeff at his office the next morning.

We arrived with a disk containing the manuscript for this book. We said to Jeff, "Show us how to use this disk in your computer." He showed us how his computer could take us to any of the ski lifts in our town so that whenever we wanted to ski we could tell which lifts were the least busy. We interrupted him: "Jeff, we don't ski. All we do is write books. Could you show us how to use our disk in your machine?" He then showed us how his computer's CD-Rom system could enhance our creativity through stereophonic music. We interrupted him again: "Jeff, we need quiet when we write. Could you show us how to use this disk?" Jeff didn't seem to understand. He told us we could do four different things at once on his

computer, including playing solitaire. We told him we like to do one thing at once and we play all the solitaire we'd ever want with Denny's mother when she comes to visit.

What we've reported here is what we understood of our three-hour visit with Jeff. Most of it was unintelligible to us and filled with words like "megahertz," "gigabytes" and "ram." Jeff assured us that we needed large quantities of this stuff or else what we bought today would certainly be obsolete tomorrow (let alone in three years when a new "information highway" would make everything we bought now totally useless).

Jeff never could get our disk working in his machine. He said our computer was "a real dinosaur" and the new equipment couldn't read our disk . . . unless we bought $300 worth of software that would get our disk to work in his machine. Then he told us that "computer prices fluctuate every day" and the cost of the computer had risen 20 percent since our phone conversation yesterday. We left with no computer and our minds totally muddled.

That evening we shared with each other our anger at feeling caught in a system that pressures us to buy more than we need and then makes things obsolete as fast as possible. We realized it wasn't only Jeff that we needed to forgive—it was our entire economic system, based as it is on competition and consumerism rather than on sharing. We talked about how difficult it is to live in our culture for even one day without being hurt by this system.

Then we recalled a recent visit to the home of our friends, Paul and Jean. We'd been looking at the computer ads in their newspaper. Paul and Jean said they were thinking of buying a new computer, too. Even though their computer was only six years old and worked fine, it was already out of date because it had no CD-Rom. Their nine-year-old son, Adam, needed a CD-Rom in order to do his homework. Because their computer was so out of date that it had no trade-in value, they would have to wait at least two years before they could afford to buy a new one. Sitting in our living room and trying to recover from our meeting with Jeff, we realized that both our friends and ourselves were being oppressed by the computer monster.

We called Paul and Jean and said, "What if you donate your worthless computer to us and we loan you the money we would have spent on a new one? Then you can buy a new computer. You can pay us back in two years." Paul and Jean loved the idea. Best of all, two days later they taught us everything we needed to know in order to get our disk to work in their computer. If we get stuck, we can always consult nine-year-old Adam.

How did we come up with this creative solution? We simply allowed ourselves to be loved with what we were feeling—with our anger and also with our fears (we will never get this book written, we will never survive in this world of computer technology) that were underneath that anger. We did not try to change or fix ourselves. In that atmosphere of staying centered in ourselves, a creative solution emerged naturally.

Looking at what happened in terms of the five stages of forgiveness, we were most aware of *anger*. Yet, today we know that we were probably in many stages simultaneously. We were in *denial* believing (despite a daily worsening prognosis) that our thirteen-year-old computer would live forever. We had *bargains* such as,

"We will forgive the world of computers only if it will make itself understandable to us, or only if it will give us what we need (not more than we need) at a price that is fair to everyone." We were also in the *depression* stage, blaming ourselves for being computer illiterates. We may have been in all five stages at once, even though we were aware of feelings and reactions relating only to the anger stage.

In the five stages of forgiveness it is not important to figure out what stage we are in or even to go through all five stages. We never said, "Oh, now we are in the anger stage." Nor did we figure out how to go through the other four stages. We simply stayed, as best we could, centered in ourselves and open to receiving love and care from each other. Whenever we do that, we will automatically move through the five stages of forgiveness.

Sometimes it *is* helpful to know what stage we are in, such as when we feel stuck or when we want to know how best to begin the process of forgiveness. However, this knowing comes most easily not by trying to figure it out, but by letting ourselves be loved in the midst of our stuckness and confusion. Nonviolence toward others begins with nonviolence toward ourselves. Nonviolence toward ourselves includes allowing each of the five chapters in the story of forgiveness to reveal itself to us in its own time.

Chapter 10

TOMATO WAR

Imagine yourself once again in the scene described in Chapter 1. On a dark, cold night you are walking home through a deserted neighborhood. Laden down with heavy packages, you hear footsteps approaching from behind. The footsteps sound like those of the men who previously beat you unconscious and then stole everything but your underwear. Knowing what you do now about Jesus' third way of creative nonviolent engagement, what would you do?

One woman in a similar situation turned around, smiled at the strangers, held out her packages and said, "I was rather nervous on this street—and these bags are so heavy. Would you help me?" Instinctively the men took the packages and walked along beside the women as she cheerfully told them how nice they were to help her.

When we first heard this story we said to one another, "How did that woman ever come up with such a wonderful solution?" According to Angie O'Gorman, the wonder-fulness of the solution is a clue to what creates a "context of conversion" in which Jesus' third way of nonviolent engagement can best succeed. It seems that the human psyche cannot be in a state of cruelty and a state of wonder simultaneously. To remain in a state of cruelty, an oppressor needs a victim who acts, in a predictable way, like a victim. Thus if the woman had responded as most victims do, with either aggression or helplessness, it would be as if she were saying to the strangers, "You're right. You are the oppressors, and I am the victim." Such predictable behavior usually affirms oppressors in their cruelty.

Wonder, however, can diffuse cruelty by breaking the predictable "You are the oppressor and I am the victim" cycle. As the woman smiles at the strangers and asks them to help carry her packages, she is no longer just a victim but a "wonder carrier." When the woman does not treat the strangers as oppressors, they are surprised—and surprise is at the heart of wonder. In such a state, "a desire to imitate tends to occur . . . that creates in the assailant a strong new impulse incompatible with the violent tendency." Thus the oppressor, too, has an opportunity to create himself anew.

Sometimes, as in the case of the woman with the packages who had little time to think, we spontaneously know how to become "wonder carriers." But what can we do when spontaneous solutions don't come to us? Sometimes we remain in hurtful situations for hours, days or years because we don't know what else to do. How can we open ourselves to discovering a creative solution consistent with Jesus' third way?

In each of the five stages of forgiveness, the oppressor becomes less of an oppressor and the victim becomes less of a victim. As this happens, wonder is possible. Thus, when we are not spontaneously aware of a solution, the five stages of forgiveness can allow one to emerge. In the story of John, because we moved too quickly through the five stages we didn't find such a solution. In the story that follows, we did find one.

THEY TOOK MY TOMATOES

Last year I (Matt) spent hours trying to raise tomatoes: pruning, fertilizing, watering and trying to arrest a tomato blight. As the green tomatoes appeared, I looked forward to the day when I could finally harvest them. But a week before harvest time I noticed that all my tomatoes had vanished. The neighbor told me he arrived too late to stop four children about eight years old who were in the midst of a tomato fight. I knew those kids because when they weren't throwing tomatoes, they were throwing glass bottles in the alley. I was sure they picked on my garden because I had asked them to stop throwing bottles.

Denial: *There's No Problem*

Usually I tend to deny hurts at first. I've learned to not express my anger because all my life whoever hurt me was taller and stronger than I am. But this time I had little problem with denial. Perhaps it was because those four eight-year-olds were actually shorter than I am. The fact is, I was furious.

Anger: *This Oppressor Is My Enemy*

The longer I looked at my tomato plants, the more I got in touch with the second stage of forgiveness, anger. I fumed, "First, it was glass. Now, it's tomatoes. Next they'll be breaking into my house. Why in only a few years these kids will be just like the pimps and drug dealers who drive their white Cadillacs up and down our street and make all of us afraid to go out at night."

I fantasized about punishing them by having them water and weed my garden in reparation. But it would be more trouble to get them to water and weed carefully than to just do it myself. Then I fantasized about going to tell their parents. Knowing their less-than-sensitive childrearing techniques, I was fairly sure these kids' parents would teach them a lesson they wouldn't soon forget. During the next week, every time I looked at my tomato-less plants I dreamed up another vengeful scheme.

I was surprised by how cruel my fantasies were. Although I didn't act out my fantasies, I did listen to them. They were saying, "You don't deserve to have your property destroyed. Don't remain a victim of these oppressors." Each fantasy filled me with the energy to protect myself, even though I didn't exactly know how I was going to do it.

Bargaining: *What Do I Need?*

The more I asked, "How am I going to protect myself and my property?" the more I entered into the third stage of forgiveness, that of bargaining. At first glance, my angry fantasies seemed to contain the bargain, "I will forgive the kids only if they get punished."

But as I cared for my anger, my real needs emerged and my bargains changed. "I will forgive them only if they apologize and promise to never do it again." Now my body felt less tense. But my body didn't totally relax until I thought, "I will forgive the kids if they learn responsibility and begin contributing something to the neighborhood." I was now closer to what I needed in order to restore my inner security and trust in others. Bargains give me the capacity to dream about what the ideal results of a creative solution might be.

Depression: *I'm a Helpless Victim*

But how could I ever get my bargains met? If I said or did anything to those kids, I thought, they would get even with me. Homes and cars were always getting broken into on our street. I was sure that if I confronted them about my tomatoes, my house and car would be next. After all, when I confronted them about broken glass, they retaliated by getting my tomatoes. I began blaming myself for ever having confronted them about the glass in the first place. I felt like a helpless victim with my hands tied by four oppressors, each only eight years old. I was now in the fourth stage of forgiveness, that of depression.

One day when I was out weeding my tomato plants, I saw that my lettuce had been harvested by slicing off the top half of each plant (the part that produced new growth) rather than just taking the outside leaves. The butchered plants would soon die. This time I discovered that the culprit was not the kids but rather Karl, a member of my Jesuit community and a good friend. Karl thought he was helping me by harvesting lettuce while I was out of town. Although I knew my lettuce plants wouldn't grow again, I forgave Karl readily.

Each morning since my tomatoes disappeared I had sat prayerfully with whatever I was feeling, letting myself be loved with those feelings. The morning after I discovered the butchered lettuce, I was reflecting on how readily I had forgiven Karl. He had done more damage to my garden than the neighborhood kids who merely picked tomatoes that would grow back. I realized that I could forgive Karl because I knew he did the best he could. Then it occurred to me that the four kids were probably doing the best they could too.

When I want to understand another's world, it helps me to try to become that person and walk in his or her shoes. When I tried to become eight years old and four feet tall, I felt helpless. Like myself, these children were victims. They were latchkey kids from single-parent families that also happened to be quite dysfunctional. Their parents felt frustrated by a social system in which they had to work two jobs and long hours just to survive. The kids were easy targets for the parents to vent their frustration. I saw that these children, full of their parents' frustration, might well see me as an oppressor. They were black. I was a white, middle class male. As such, I symbolized to many poor black people what kept an unjust social system going. Perhaps the kids experienced me as the oppressive "boss man" each time I asked them to clean up the glass bottles they had broken. Just as they saw

me as "boss man," I had projected onto them my anger at feeling oppressed by the neighborhood drug dealers. As I walked in the shoes of the four kids, I realized that we were all both oppressors and victims, and that we were all doing the best we could.

Sometimes misbehavior is the best we can do. Children tend to misbehave when they lose their sense of belonging. Their misbehavior gets the attention of adults, and for emotionally starved children even negative attention is better than no attention at all. The four neighborhood kids had probably learned from my reaction to the broken glass that I paid the most attention to them when they caused trouble. Stealing my tomatoes might be the best way they knew to get more attention from me.

Also, we all want others to understand how we feel. When children (or adults) have feelings they don't know how to verbalize, they will often unconsciously try to produce those same feelings in others. This, too, is a desperate way of trying to connect with other human beings and regain a sense of belonging. Perhaps these four children who felt so frustrated and helpless were trying to produce the same feelings in me. Again, their misbehavior was the best way they knew to get what they needed.

I saw that I was just like the four children. I didn't know how to tell them how upset I was about losing my tomatoes and so I had cruel fantasies about hurting them so they would feel as bad as I felt. I thought, "The only reason I don't often try to hurt others is because I have a lot of people who love me and listen to me. Those kids have no one."

The depression stage invites us to walk in the shoes of our oppressor to see what we might have done differently before, during, or after the hurtful situation. The more I did this and the more I realized that all of us were doing the best we could, I no longer felt so distant from the children. I began to see the good in them. After all, throwing tomatoes was a definite improvement over throwing bottles, which had ceased when I asked them to stop. If they were really trying to harm me, they would have thrown the tomatoes at my house (maybe even through a window) rather than at each other. I felt able to forgive them because I saw that, like Karl,

the kids were doing the best they could. I had a greater desire to connect and be one with them, but I still wasn't sure how.

I recalled my bargains: I wanted the four children to learn responsibility and contribute something to the neighborhood. A week later I saw the kids cutting through my yard. I consciously tried to see them as good kids doing the best they could rather than as enemies. Holding this attitude in my heart, I called them over. First I thanked them for not throwing any more bottles in the alley. Then I said,

> You know those tomatoes I've been trying so hard to grow? I found them in the neighbor's yard, all smashed. He told me he saw some kids having a tomato fight. I don't know who did it. I'm hoping you would be willing to protect my garden and share the tomatoes when they're ripe. If no more tomatoes disappear, each of you can have all the tomatoes from one plant. What do you think?

They looked thoroughly surprised that I was giving out tomatoes rather than vindictive punishment. With their faces still full of wonder, they each eagerly chose a tomato plant to be responsible for. From then on my garden had great protection and no more tomatoes disappeared. The kids became my friends and even showed up one time to help me water their plants.

Acceptance: *We Are Equals*

By now I could easily forgive the four children for stealing my tomatoes. I was grateful for the whole experience because it taught me how marauding enemies can change into gardening friends. This is acceptance, the fifth stage of forgiveness in which we can be grateful for the good that has come out of the hurt.

But what if things hadn't worked out so well? Or, what if next week the kids break into my house? The five stages of forgiveness do not guarantee that we will always come up with a creative solution nor that the creative solution will always work. Moreover, forgiveness is not the same as reconciliation, and the five stages

We are equals !!

do not guarantee that the person who hurt us will respond in a way that makes reconciliation possible.

What the stages *do* guarantee is that *we* will be different as we forgive. I was fairly certain that I would never again see the children only as oppressors and myself as only a victim. In the acceptance stage, what mattered was not whether my creative solution of inviting the kids to guard my tomatoes worked or not. What mattered was that I no longer divided people into oppressors and victims but rather realized that the kids and I all belong to the same human family. Ultimately, *this* is the creative solution to every hurt and conflict.

Stage	*Signs of a Creative Solution Emerging*
DENIAL	I let myself be loved until I am ready to face the pain of the hurt. Gradually I stop pretending that nothing happened and begin caring for my hurt as I recognize that you are an oppressor and I am a victim.
ANGER	I want to change you so you are not an oppressor and I am not a victim. As I move through anger, I gradually consider you less as my oppressor and more as an essentially good person, capable of wonder and worthy of compassion.
BARGAINING	I discover what you need in order to stop being an oppressor and what I need in order to stop being a victim.
DEPRESSION	I want to change myself so I am not a helpless victim. As my guilt and shame heal, I gradually feel less like a helpless victim and more like an essentially good (but fallible) wonder carrier worthy of respect.
ACCEPTANCE	Whether I discover a creative solution or not, and whether it works or not, I will no longer treat you only as an oppressor nor myself only as a victim.

THE TWO HANDS OF FORGIVENESS

What Matt learned in the story of the tomato war might be summarized with Barbara Deming's image of the two hands of nonviolence, introduced in Chapter 2. As she describes it, we have two hands upon the oppressor, "one hand taking from him what is not his due, the other slowly calming

him as we do this." Thus, with one hand we stop the oppressor from abusing us by refusing our cooperation, by saying "No, you may not steal my tomatoes." At the same moment we hold out the other hand to offer the oppressor a sense of belonging, saying, "You are not the other and I am not the other. No one is the other. . . . I won't let go of you or cast you out of the human race. I have faith that you can make a better choice than you are making now, and I'll be here when you're ready."

This second hand, which reaches out to offer the oppressor a sense of belonging, is essential because wonder and cruelty cannot coexist. Wonder happens at moments when we are surprised by the astonishing inner coherence and unity of all things. Wonder is rooted in a sense of connectedness, the connectedness which is the fundamental truth of the universe. When we feel wonder, we cannot be cruel to any part of life because we know it all belongs to us and we to it. This wonder and sense of belonging are hallmarks of the acceptance stage.

The five stages of forgiveness can help us find wonder-ful creative solutions because they help us avoid getting stuck in "You are the other, you are an oppressor, you don't belong" (the anger stage) or "I am the other, I am a victim, I don't belong" (the depression stage). The recognition that no one is the other and that we all belong helps us resist returning violence in kind or allowing ourselves to be abused. From our penal system to international relations, this principle seems little understood.

Yet, as Matt discovered, small children instinctively understand it and good parenting protects them from forgetting it. As soon-to-be-new-parents we (Sheila & Dennis) notice the common denominator in all the best parenting literature we can find: set firm limits on children and don't deny them the consequences of their behavior (don't be a victim), but don't punish them or try to overpower them (don't be an oppressor either). When children misbehave, such as by stealing tomatoes, we can offer them the two hands of forgiveness and nonviolence. One hand says, "I will not accept this behavior," and the other says, "You belong to me and together we can find a better way for both of us to get our needs met." For those of us who were not raised in this way, the five stages are a form of reparenting and hope-fully can become a way of life.

Chapter 11

THE FIVE STAGES & NONVIOLENT ENGAGEMENT AS A WAY OF LIFE

We began the last chapter with the story of a woman who spontaneously knew how to become one with her oppressors by asking them to carry her packages. For her, the lesson of the five stages had become a way of life. She instinctively avoided dividing people into oppressors and victims. She was able to simultaneously maintain her dignity and disarm the two men who were about to assault her. She saw the best in them and offered them a sense of belonging.

I (Dennis) learned the importance of the five stages as a way of life several years ago while I was living in an inner city Jesuit community in Omaha. I woke up one night and realized there was a man in my room. In the dark he looked like Tim, a Jesuit whom I hadn't seen for a while. I thought maybe Tim was staying overnight with us on his way through Omaha, and perhaps had wandered into the wrong room. Still half asleep, I said, "The corner room is empty. And if you're hungry, there's ham in the refrigerator."

I was about to fall back asleep when I realized that Tim lived nine hundred miles away. If he was coming to visit I probably would have been the first one he told. I sat straight up in bed and thought, "I just offered our ham to a thief!" I raced down to the kitchen. The ham was safe. I called two other Jesuits on the kitchen intercom and together we searched the house. The thief was gone and so was one of our bicycles.

I went back to my room and locked the door. I tried to go back to sleep but couldn't. Then I realized what was wrong. I got up and unlocked my bedroom door. I fell asleep immediately.

I was dividing my world into victims and oppressors.....

I knew the reason I couldn't go to sleep at first was because I had just locked my bedroom door for the first time in my entire life. As long as my door was locked, I was dividing my world into victims and oppressors. When I unlocked my door, I restored a world in which everyone belonged. This world of belonging had given me a creative solution that probably saved me from harm at the hands of a thief: I greeted him as a friend.

Chapter 12

THE CHILDHOOD ROOTS OF NONVIOLENCE

Even after all that we have said about the five stages of forgiveness, you may still wonder how your first response in a threatening situation could ever be creative nonviolence. Perhaps you cannot imagine yourself, in a calm and friendly voice, asking two threatening strangers to help carry your packages, or telling a thief, "If you're hungry there's ham in the refrigerator." Perhaps you can only imagine yourself either cowering in fear or striking out in anger.

These responses can feel so deep as to seem instinctual. Yet we suspect that in fact they are learned in childhood. If this is true, then a creative nonviolent response in threatening situations can also be learned in childhood. Our hope is that this too can feel so deep as to seem instinctual. For example, those who risked their lives to rescue Jews during the Holocaust have been studied extensively. When asked why they did it, many rescuers say something like, "I couldn't imagine doing otherwise. In our family we children were always treated with kindness. We were taught to see all people as deserving that same kindness. How could I not reach out to help the Jews?"

In Chapter 2 we gave examples of nonviolence and forgiveness, ranging from parenting to politics. We included parenting because we believe parenting that offers children the two hands of nonviolence is the foundation of the capacity for nonviolence in later life. Our eight-year-old friend Tom experienced this when he began kindergarten at St. John's School. Andy Jones was one of the most popular teachers at the school. He was also well known and loved in the wider community. Andy was out with his friends at a bar one evening and had too much to drink. The bartender asked him to leave and Andy angrily objected. He went home, got his handgun, returned to the bar and shot the bouncer. Andy was arrested and charged with aggravated assault.

The next day the pastor of St. John's announced a meeting of the whole school. The parents, who had read about Andy in the morning newspaper, were invited. The pastor asked the children if they knew what Mr. Jones had done. Then she asked them how they felt about Mr. Jones. The children expressed feelings of anger, disapproval and disappointment. They said they thought what Mr. Jones did was very bad. The pastor said, "I feel angry too and I don't like what he did either." Obviously confused, the children said, "But we still love him. How can we still love him when he did something so bad?" Crying visibly, the pastor said, "I still love Mr. Jones too."

Then she asked the children if any of them had ever done anything they regarded as very bad. All the children nodded. The pastor asked if they thought their parents still loved them when they did something bad. Most of the children said "Yes."

The pastor pointed to Mr. Jones' parents, who were sitting in the front row, and said,

Mr. Jones' parents still love him, too. I believe that's how God feels toward all of us when we do something bad. We need to love Mr. Jones, even though we don't like what he did. I suggest we love him by writing letters to him and by praying for him while he is in jail. I'll visit him and bring the letters myself. How many of you want to help?

All the children volunteered and they have continued to write letters and pray for Mr. Jones ever since.

Unlike the children at St. John's, many of us learned to see ourselves as good and loved when we pleased our parents, and as bad and not quite so loved (or hardly loved at all) when we displeased our parents. Thus we split ourselves into a "good" self and a "bad" self. If we regard ourselves in this way, how can we possibly regard others any differently? If our inner life is a struggle between a victim and an oppressor, how natural and even instinctive it would seem to either cower before others in fear or strike out at them in anger.

Conversely, when we treat others as belonging to us no matter what they do, we heal the split within ourselves. The connectedness to all of life that is intrinsic to wonder and that abolishes cruelty begins within.

By reminding the children of times when they had received unconditional love despite misbehavior, the pastor of St. John's evoked their capacity to remain connected to Mr. Jones. And by encouraging the children to remain connected to Mr. Jones, she was encouraging them to remain connected to all the misbehaving parts of themselves. These children are unlikely to split themselves into "good" and "bad," and therefore unlikely to divide the world into "good guys" and "bad guys." Creative nonviolent solutions to conflicts in later life are likely to come naturally to them.

The rest of us may need to apply the five stage process of forgiveness to any parts of ourselves that we learned to see as bad, and to anyone who taught us to see ourselves in this way by failing to love us unconditionally. And we may need to return again and again to moments when we were loved unconditionally, or when we witnessed unconditional love. As we take those moments in, they can gradually empower us to love unconditionally like Tom and his classmates at St. John's.

Part II:
HEALING PROCESSES

The following two chapters each contain a healing process that we have often used to help us move through the five stages of forgiveness. Chapter 13 contains "Focusing Prayer," which invites us to listen to God speaking within our bodies. Chapter 14 contains the "Emmaus Prayer," which invites us to listen to God speaking to us through the scriptures.

FOCUSING PRAYER

Recently we received an angry letter from friends whom we'll call Steve and Angela. They were upset about our new book, *Good Goats: Healing Our Image of God.* Although we appreciated that Steve and Angela wrote directly to us rather than to several hundred other people, in some ways their letter reminded us of John. For example, they not only disagreed with our theology but also criticized us personally by suggesting that we were under the influence of evil. Their letter also reminded us of John because *Good Goats* was a more developed version of the same basic ideas that he had criticized in our earlier tape. We had spent the intervening years studying and revising this material, so that we would be better able to respond to people like John.

Several years ago we were easily shaken by John's criticism and we needed a lot of reassurance from theologians and from the Christian community. By the time Steve and Angela wrote to us, we were far more confident of our position. We knew *Good Goats* was well within the parameters of orthodox Roman Catholic theology. We had endorsements from highly respected theologians, the book was on our publisher's best-seller list, and it would go on to win a Catholic Press Association Book Award. This time we weren't worried that we had made a mistake, or that Steve and Angela would damage our reputation.

However, we felt hurt by the harshness of their letter. And, like the good children that the three of us are often tempted to be, when we are criticized we want to satisfy our critics' objections. Our first thought was to write a letter back in which we would answer all Steve and Angela's criticisms with theological evidence for our point of view. In other words, we would overpower them . . . with words.

Then, one afternoon I (Sheila) was rereading Steve and Angela's letter and a rough draft of our response. Something seemed wrong with our response, but

I didn't know what. I noticed that my shoulders were hunched over and my breathing was shallow. I stopped reading, closed my eyes and let my awareness down further into my body, listening for what it was trying to say to me. I had an image of something large and oppressive trying to envelop me, from which my body was shrinking away. As I let myself down into that shrinking feeling, I heard the word "shame." At that moment I realized that Steve and Angela's letter was not about theology. It was about shame. It was about a shame-based model of Christianity in which people are not intrinsically ok. Rather, they are ok only if they hold certain beliefs and definitely not ok if they hold differing beliefs.

Then I knew what was wrong with our response to Steve and Angela. We were responding as if the issue were a theological disagreement, when really the issue was the shaming and disrespectful nature of their letter. As we had with John, we were denying the *real* hurt. Steve and Angela were telling us we weren't ok because of our theology, and we were using theological arguments to prove we *were* ok. Their shame-based model of Christianity was emotionally violent. In a sense, we were returning violence in kind by trying to overpower them with theological arguments. If we sent the response we had prepared, we would be cooperating with their shaming behavior toward us, and spending a lot of our time and energy to do it. Moreover, we would only reinforce their worldview in which ok-ness depends on "right" beliefs.

The awareness came to me that we could discuss theology with Steve and Angela only if the starting point were that we and they were all ok. I recalled a friend's comment that "God loves us all a lot more than God loves our theology." At this, my whole body relaxed, my shoulders straightened, my chest felt open and I began breathing normally. My body knew I was on the track of a creative solution that avoided both responding with violence (anger) and taking abuse by cooperating with shaming behavior (depression). Staying with that relaxed and open bodily feeling, I composed a letter that matched it.

In this letter I thanked Steve and Angela for coming to us first. I told them that there was a long tradition for their point of view, and a long tradition for ours as well. We were not lost and neither were they. I asked them to write back to us in a way that focused on the issues rather than questioning our personal characters or our relationship with God. I shared this letter with Dennis and Matt and we agreed to mail it.

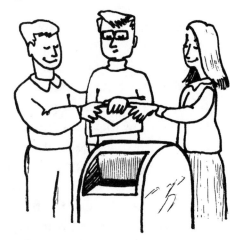

The process of listening to my body that I have just described is known as "focusing." We mentioned earlier that each of the five stages is like a chapter in a story. The focusing process is a way of allowing the story to unfold, especially as it wants to unfold through our bodies. Thus, for me the story began to unfold as I noticed that my shoulders were hunched over and my breathing was shallow. I know now that my body was alerting me to the fact that I was stuck in the depression stage.

As I allowed my body to continue telling its story, I heard its underlying message: "We don't have to prove we're ok." With this, my whole body could relax. Such a felt body shift is an indication that we have heard at least part of the message that our body wants to communicate. It is as if our body is breathing a sigh of relief and saying, "Thanks for listening."

As my chest opened and I began breathing normally, I sensed that I had let go of the temptation to divide people into victims and oppressors. I felt centered in myself and equal to Steve and Angela. Thus a creative solution could emerge. As the solution emerged in the form of a letter, I set aside any ideas that brought back the feeling of shallow breathing and followed ideas that seemed to enhance that open bodily feeling.

There is no guarantee that focusing or our creative solutions will change the other person. Steve and Angela never wrote back to us, and so we do not know what effect our letter had upon them. But we do know the effect it had upon us: we no longer fear angry letters from people who disagree with our theology. We now know that we do not need to let others shame us with their criticisms, nor do we need to vanquish them with our response. In other words, we are less likely to get stuck in either the depression stage (I'm not ok) or the anger stage (you're not ok).

In this experience, my body knew the truth that we are all ok and we all deserve to be treated with respect. When I was tempted to deviate from this truth, my body was full of dis-ease. When I was on the track of a creative solution that expressed this truth, my body relaxed.

In focusing we will automatically move through the stages of forgiveness as our bodies keep confirming for us the next step that God is inviting us to take. Focusing helps us discover how grace, or the action of God, feels in our body. Following are the steps:

FOCUSING PRAYER PROCESS

1. Imagine yourself in the presence of someone who loves you, such as God or your best friend. Take some deep breaths and fill your body with that love.
2. Sit comfortably with your eyes closed. Let your awareness move down into the center of your body and notice what you feel there.
3. Get in touch with a hurt for which you still need healing.

4. Ask yourself if you *want* to listen to this part of yourself right now. Is it ok to spend some time with it? If not, care for the feeling of not wanting to spend time with this right now.

5. If it is ok to spend some time with this area of your life, take a few moments to create a loving atmosphere where it will feel safe to speak to you. For example, how would you prepare your home if your best friend were coming to visit? How would you reach out to a hurting child or a wounded pet?

6. Now let yourself down into how this whole thing feels inside you. Where in your body do you especially experience it? Perhaps you feel an ache in your chest, a lump in your throat, a knot in your stomach, shaking in your legs, etc.

7. Care for this feeling and see if it wants to tell you about itself, perhaps through a word, an image or a symbol. Perhaps it wants to come to you as a little child. Perhaps it wants to tell you its name, its history (when and how it developed) and what it needs.

8. Whatever comes, reach out to care for it without trying to change it or fix it. Or, maybe just put your hand on that part of your body in a caring way. If you wish, ask Jesus, God as you understand God, or some other trusted person to come and help you care for it.

9. Notice how your body feels now compared to when you began. Are you now carrying the hurtful situation differently in your body? For example, do you feel more relaxed, open, light, etc.? If so, see if any creative solution to the hurtful situation occurs naturally to you that is consistent with this relaxed, open, light, etc. feeling.

10. Whatever you are feeling, before concluding tell this part of you that you will come back at another time to listen to it and care for it some more.

Chapter 14

EMMAUS PRAYER

The story of Emmaus in Luke 24:13–35 is Jesus' ultimate story of turning the other cheek. In the midst of the cruelest crucifixion and death, he found a creative solution.

Jesus walks along the road to Emmaus with two hopeless, depressed disciples. For some reason, perhaps because they are so discouraged, they do not even recognize Jesus. They are depressed not only because they think their great prophet, Jesus, is dead, but also because their hopes, "all that the great prophet said and did," are also dead. Jesus had taught nonviolent resistance against cruel authority. The two disciples' "own hope had been that Jesus would be the one to set Israel free" from such authority. But instead, Jesus' nonviolent resistance had ultimately led those same authorities "to hand him over to be sentenced and to have him crucified." For the two disciples, not only had Jesus died but his way of nonviolent resistance had died too. Violence had won.

As Jesus walks the road to Emmaus with these two disciples, he allows them to share this great hurt. They begin by sharing how the chief priests and leaders are clearly the oppressors and how they are clearly the victims. However, as Jesus takes them through the five stages of forgiveness, the clear line between who is oppressor and who is victim fades. As this happens, Jesus is then ready to help them discover a creative solution.

First, Jesus invites the disciples to share their hurt as he takes them through the five stages. The two disciples begin by refusing to let anyone, even Jesus, remain in the stage of denial. "You must be the only person staying in Jerusalem who does not know the things that have been happening there these last few days." It's almost as if the disciples want to shake Jesus out of the denial in which they imagine him to be. They accuse him of being naive, "the only person" who does not know the obvious.

The two disciples then share their anger about what the chief priests and leaders did, and about how Jesus let them down. And if all that weren't enough, they don't know what to make of those women who couldn't find Jesus' body in the tomb. The women claimed to have seen a vision of angels who had declared Jesus was alive. But when the disciples sent their friends to verify this report, their friends hadn't found any evidence that Jesus was alive.

We can only guess at what the two disciples' bargains were. But judging from the outcome of the story, one bargain may have been, "I will forgive Jesus, the women, the chief priests and leaders, only if the report that Jesus is alive is true."

In the depression stage, Jesus listens to all that the disciples want to share about why they feel hopeless. But he doesn't push them. Perhaps the disciples are secretly blaming themselves for abandoning Jesus so quickly. They may have often wondered, "Why didn't we stick by Jesus in his last hours? Why did we hand Jesus over to death so readily?" When the disciples report that the chief priest and leaders put Jesus to death, perhaps they are trying to justify themselves by saying, "It's all their fault." Yet, Jesus doesn't push the disciples to face what they are not yet ready to face.

At the end of the story, the two disciples reflect on how the acceptance stage happened gradually. "Did not our hearts begin to burn within us as he talked to us on the road and explained the scriptures to us?" Somehow "to make their hearts burn" Jesus must have first of all communicated to them that he understood their hurt. Then he probably explained to them the various scriptures that spoke to what made them so angry and depressed. As they felt loved in their weakness, they would have become more able to love other weak human beings as well. The division between who was victim and who was oppressor was swallowed up in a sense of oneness with all humanity. They felt such unity with this stranger that when they arrived at the disciples' village and he wanted to go on, they insisted he stay with them.

That feeling of oneness made them open to the creative solution: the breaking of the bread. As "Jesus sat with them at table, he took the bread and said the blessing; then he broke it and handed it to them. And their eyes were opened and they recognized him."

They couldn't believe it. Jesus was offering them bread. They who had disappeared and abandoned Jesus rather than die, they were being fed by Jesus. The bread had changed everything. It was as if Jesus was saying, "There are no longer oppressors or victims. We all belong." The breaking of the bread was Jesus' way of nonviolent engagement, his sign of the equality of all human beings. It worked. It transformed the disciples. Perhaps it was because they could stop blaming themselves, perhaps it was because their hope was restored. Whatever it was, because of the bread they felt so different that "their eyes were opened and they recognized him."

The two disciples were so energized by the experience of breaking bread that they changed their plans. Instead of spending the night in Emmaus, "they set out that instant and returned to Jerusalem." They had to tell their friends immediately "what had happened on the road and how they had recognized Jesus at the breaking of the bread."

The two disciples' story was so convincing that for many centuries, not just in Jerusalem but everywhere Christians went, they continued to celebrate Jesus' third way of nonviolent engagement, the breaking of the bread. They did it just as Jesus did—with outcasts, sinners, with their very enemies—until they felt one with all people. Even today, just like the two disciples, each time we experience the breaking of the bread we can be assured that Jesus is alive and that his way of nonviolence will ultimately win.

Two important things happened in the Emmaus story. First of all, Jesus walked the two disciples through the five stages of forgiveness. Like the disciples, any of us will automatically move through the stages of forgiveness if we have a significant other with whom we can share all our feelings. Secondly, as the clear lines between oppressor and victim faded, Jesus gave the disciples a creative solution: the bread, as an enduring symbol of human oneness and equality. In the prayer that follows, we invite you to let Jesus walk you through the five stages of forgiveness.

EMMAUS PRAYER

1. Read the story of the disciples on the road to Emmaus (Lk 24:13–35).
2. Imagine yourself walking down the dirt road to Emmaus with Jesus. Maybe even feel the dirt between your toes. Like the two disciples, share with Jesus a hurt in your life. Tell Jesus what was said and done that made the situation so painful.
3. When you have shared all your feelings, let Jesus tell you how he feels about what happened to you. Watch what he says and does for you. Take some deep breaths and take in all the love that he wants to give you.
4. Repeat steps 2 and 3 as often as needed until you feel completely cared for and understood. Take as long as you wish. There is no need to move on to the next step.

5. If you feel drawn to do so, watch what Jesus says and does for the person who hurt you. Take some deep breaths. Each time you exhale, help Jesus fill that person with life.

6. Finally, ask Jesus to show you if there is some creative way of nonviolent engagement that will protect you and invite the person who hurt you to conversion as well. You may get some clues as to what Jesus might invite you to do by recalling what Jesus said and did for you or for the other person.

One reader of an early version of this book expressed skepticism that nonviolent engagement could ever really win in this world. For anyone who reads a newspaper, it's easy enough to appreciate her point of view. Sometimes it seems that we have learned very little from all our centuries of war, and that violence is only increasing. Yet the three of us want to hold out the hope that something really is changing in our world. As Gil Bailie says in his remarkable book *Violence Unveiled*, it's only now after two thousand years that the example of Jesus' life and death is making violence no longer a viable solution to human problems and conflicts.

Where two hundred years ago murderers were publicly hanged as entertainment for spectators, today we agonize over capital punishment. Parenting programs are offering a whole new way of raising children based on democratic principles rather than on authoritarianism and punishment. Wars are still being fought in many places in the world. Yet more and more of our military efforts involve humanitarian and peacekeeping projects (albeit often for motives of self-interest) rather than aggression.

Perhaps we feel hope because we just returned from giving retreats in the Philippines. We stayed in a home just a few blocks from EDSA, the nickname for the main street of Manila. This was the site of the 1986 revolution that overthrew the dictatorship of Ferdinand Marcos. Known as the EDSA Revolution, it was entirely nonviolent. The revolution began when a small faction of Marcos' army became so disillusioned with his government that they asked Cardinal Sin for help. Cardinal Sin went on the radio and asked all the people to go out into the streets and peacefully protest the Marcos regime. Millions of people lined EDSA, many of them participating in Catholic Masses that were celebrated on nearly every street corner.

All our Filipino friends remember where they were during those days. Marta told us, "I packed a lunch and brought my four children to join the people at EDSA. We brought extra food for the soldiers. Government helicopters flew over us. I knew we could be killed. But the spirit of the people was so full of life that I had to be part of it."

As Marcos' tanks moved toward the crowds, the people surrounded them and offered flowers, rosaries and food to the soldiers. The soldiers, apparently overcome by such an outpouring of love and forgiveness, climbed out of the tanks and joined the people.

The EDSA Revolution lasted only four days, but it was the fruit of years of preparation. Teams from the United States and elsewhere had trained local communities in nonviolence. By the time the tanks rolled toward the people, enough of them had learned to extend the two hands of forgiveness that the soldiers were converted to a new way of responding. Today, the former rebel leader Honaisan and Imelda Marcos (wife of the former dictator) are both democratically elected members of the Philippine Senate.

The Philippine republic still has many economic and social problems. But the people have learned something they will never forget: when someone hits us on the right cheek, we don't need to passively let ourselves be hit on the left cheek and we don't have to hit back. Instead we can offer our oppressor the two hands of forgiveness and nonviolence, "one hand taking from him what is not his due, the other slowly calming him as we do this." We believe this creative third way can become instinctive by practicing the five stages of forgiveness as a way of life.

Page iv

Dennis & Matthew Linn, *Healing Life's Hurts: Healing Memories through the Five Stages of Forgiveness* (Mahwah, NJ: Paulist Press, 1978). The style of this book is more scholarly than the present one, and it includes extensive footnotes.

Page 1

Based upon a letter from Sheena Duncan to Walter Wink, November 6, 1989. Cited in Walter Wink, *Engaging the Powers: Discernment and Resistance in a World of Domination* (Minneapolis: Fortress Press, 1992), p. 235.

Pages 5–8

Walter Wink, *Engaging the Powers: Discernment and Resistance in a World of Domination, op. cit.* The exegesis of Matthew 5:38–42 is in Chapter 9, "Jesus' Third Way: Nonviolent Engagement," and discusses how Jesus' example of nonviolent engagement can overthrow the domination system under which we live and bring a new world order. This book has been widely acclaimed and is one of the best we have ever read. A simplified, shorter version will be published in 1997 by Doubleday, tentatively titled *The Powers that Be.* Although we find Dr. Wink's interpretation of Matthew 5:38–42 convincing, not all scripture scholars agree. For a different opinion, see Jan Lambrecht, S.J., "The Sayings of Jesus on Nonviolence," *Louvain Studies,* Vol. 12 (1987), pp. 291–305, and Jan Lambrecht, S.J., "Is Active Nonviolent Resistance Jesus' Third Way?: An Answer to Walter Wink," *Louvain Studies,* Vol. 19 (1994), pp. 350–351.

Page 7

Quote is from Wink, *op. cit.*, p. 179.

Page 9

Barbara Deming, *Prisons that Could Not Hold: Prison Notes 1964–Seneca 1984* (San Francisco: Spinsters Ink, 1985), and Jane Meyerding (ed.), *We Are All Part of One Another: A Barbara Deming Reader* (Philadelphia: New Society, 1984). Cited in Pam McAllister, *You Can't Kill the Spirit* (Philadelphia: New Society, 1988), pp. 6–7.

Page 10

Session 5, "Winning Cooperation," of the PBS television series *Active Parenting Today for Parents of Two to Twelve-Year-Olds*, by Michael Popkin (Marietta, GA: Active Parenting Publishers, 1993).

Page 13

Kathleen Hurley & Theodore Dobson, *What's My Type?* (San Francisco: Harper-Collins, 1991), p. 122.

Page 14

Dorothy Samuel, *Safe Passage on City Streets* (Richmond, IN: Liberty Literary Works, 1991), p. 86.

Page 16

Creation Spirituality, Vol. 11, No. 1 (Spring, 1995), p. 8.

Pages 19–20

Barbara Sofer, "Not in Our Town," *Woman's Day* (November 22, 1994), pp. 34–40.

Page 21

Newsweek, June 5, 1995, p. 10.

Page 23

For the story of the rescue of the Jews in Denmark, see Philip Friedman, *Their Brothers' Keepers* (New York: Crown Publishers, 1957), Chapter 12. The quote from Eichmann is found in Ron Sider & Richard K. Taylor, "International Aggression and Nonmilitary Defense," *Christian Century 100* (July 6–13, 1983), p. 645. Cited in Wink, *op. cit.*, p. 255.

Page 24

On Hitler and nonviolent engagement, Wink, *op. cit.*, pp. 254–255. For statistics for nonviolent revolutions, Wink, *op. cit.*, p. 264.

Page 28

Elisabeth Kübler-Ross, *On Death and Dying* (New York: Macmillan, 1969).

Pages 37–38

The study of metastatic breast cancer patients is by Dr. David Spiegel at Stanford University. Reported in Bill Moyers, *Healing and the Mind* (New York: Doubleday, 1993), pp. 67–68. The story of coalminers is from Deepak Chopra, "Body, Mind and Soul: The Myth & the Magic" (PBS television series, August 17, 1995).

Page 43

The concept of the "enlightened witness" comes from Alice Miller and is developed in her book *Banished Knowledge* (New York: Doubleday, 1990).

Page 46

The study of hostility and cardiac disease is by Dr. Redford Williams at Duke University. Reported in *Psychology Today* (July, 1992), p. 18. The research on exceptional cancer patients is by Bernie Siegel, reported in his book *Peace, Love & Healing* (New York: Harper, 1989). The significance of the question, "Do you want to live to be one hundred?" is on page 46.

Pages 57–58

The study of AIDS patients is by Dr. George Solomon. Reported in Bernie Siegel, *Peace, Love & Healing, op. cit.*, pp. 162–163. The study of unconditional love and immunoglobulin A is by Dr. David McClelland, reported in Larry Dossey, *Healing Words* (San Francisco: Harper, 1993), pp. 109–110.

Pages 66–67

The research on Monday as the most frequent time of death was reported by the American Heart Association (November, 1992), in *Newsweek* (December 2, 1985), p. 82, and in *U.S. News & World Report* (January 21, 1985), p. 68. The characteristics of those prone to heart attacks and the beneficial effects of sharing in a group studied by Dr. Carl Thorensen of Stanford University were reported in *The New York Times* (September 20, 1990), p. B-8.

Pages 67–68

The life review during a near death experience is described by Raymond Moody in a talk given with Melvin Morse, "Near Death Experiences" (Boulder, CO: Sounds True Recordings, 1991). Dr. Moody's comments are in response to a question as to whether he has ever encountered a "hellish" near death experience. Dr. Moody responds that in his study of over 2,500 near death experiences, he has never found anyone who actually experienced hell. He *has* encountered two cases of people who had hellish experiences while they were delirious. Delirium is quite different from an NDE. In delirium reality is distorted, whereas in an NDE reality is clearer and more real than ever before. Dr. Moody then goes on to describe the life review, by way of saying that unloving behavior *does* have consequences, but these consequences do not include hell or punishment.

Page 77

The health benefits of husbands kissing their wives before going to work was reported in *La Nacion* (San Jose, Costa Rica, February 13, 1988), p. 4.

Page 86

The story of the woman who gave strangers her packages is from Dorothy Samuel, *op. cit.*, p. 85.

Page 87

Angie O'Gorman on wonder and a context of conversion is cited in Wink, *op. cit.*, pp. 233–234. The quote is from page 234. See Angie O'Gorman, "Defense through Disarmament: Nonviolence and Personal Assault," in Angie O'Gorman (ed.), *The Universe Bends Toward Justice* (Philadelphia: New Society Publishers, 1990), pp. 241–247.

Page 96

Barbara Deming, *op. cit.*

Pages 100–101

For research on rescuers of Jews during the Holocaust, see Samuel & Pearl Oliner, *The Altruistic Personality: Rescuers of Jews in Nazi Europe* (New York: Macmillan, 1988), especially Chapter 10, "Moral Heroism and Extensivity," pp. 249–260.

Pages 109–111

Focusing was originally developed by Eugene Gendlin at the University of Chicago. See his book *Focusing* (New York: Bantam, 1978). We learned focusing from Peter Campbell and Edwin McMahon, who have integrated it with Christian spirituality, and we have built upon their method. We are indebted to Pete and Ed for the idea (paraphrased on p. 110), that "Discernment is how grace feels in the body." For an excellent brief introduction to focusing, see Peter Campbell, "Focusing: Doorway to the Body-Life of Spirit," *Creation Spirituality* (May/June, 1991), pp. 24, 26, 27, 50, 52. For a listing of books and retreats on focusing, contact Institute for Bio-Spiritual Research, P.O. Box 741137, Arvada, CO 80006-1137.

RESOURCES FOR FURTHER GROWTH BY THE AUTHORS

BOOKS

Healing Life's Hurts (1978, revised 1993). Contains a thorough discussion of the five stages of dying and how they apply to the process of forgiveness. This is our most complete resource on forgiveness, and we recommend it to readers who want to go through the process in greater depth.

Sleeping with Bread: Holding What Gives You Life (1995). A simple process—for individuals and for families and others to share—of reflecting on each day's consolation and desolation. This process can help us get in touch each day with both hurts and healing, guide our decisions and find the purpose of our life.

Healing Spiritual Abuse & Religious Addiction (1994). Why does religion help some people grow in wholeness, yet seem to make others become more rigid and stuck? Discusses religious addiction and spiritual abuse, and offers ways of healing the shame-based roots of these behaviors. Includes how spiritual abuse can also be sexually abusive, and how scripture has often been used to reinforce religious addiction and spiritual abuse. Concludes with an image of healthy religion, in which we are free to do what Jesus would do.

Good Goats: Healing Our Image of God (1994). We become like the God we adore, and if our God is shaming, abusive and violent, we are more likely to shame and abuse ourselves and/or others and less likely to find creative nonviolent solutions. One of the easiest ways to heal ourselves and our society is to heal our image of God, so that we know a God who loves us at least as much as those who love us the most. Discusses whether God throws us into hell or otherwise vengefully punishes us, and the role of free will. Includes a question and answer section that gives the theological and scriptural foundation for the main text.

Belonging: Bonds of Healing & Recovery (1993). Twelve Step recovery from any compulsive pattern is integrated with contemporary spirituality and psychology. Defines addiction as rooted in abuse and as our best attempt to belong to ourselves, others, God and the universe. This book helps the reader discover the genius underneath every addiction.

Healing the Eight Stages of Life (1988). Based on Erik Erikson's developmental system, this book helps to heal hurts and develop gifts at each stage of life, from conception through old age. Includes healing ways our image of God has been formed and deformed at each stage.

Healing of Memories (1974). A simple guide to inviting Jesus into our painful memories to help us forgive ourselves and others.

Healing the Greatest Hurt (1985). Healing the deepest hurt most people experience, the loss of a loved one, by learning to give and receive love with the deceased through the Communion of Saints.

These and other books by the authors are available from Paulist Press, 997 Macarthur Blvd., Mahwah, NJ 07430, Phone orders (800) 218-1903, FAX orders (800) 836-3161.

TAPES & COURSES *(for use alone, with a companion, or with a group)*

Good Goats: Healing Our Image of God (1994). Two-part videotape to accompany book (see above).

Healing Our Image of God (1994). Set of two audio tapes that may be used to accompany *Good Goats: Healing Our Image of God* and/or *Healing Spiritual Abuse & Religious Addiction.* Parts I and II are available from Christian Video Library; Part I only is available from Credence Cassettes under the title *Good Goats: Healing Our Image of God.*

Healing Spiritual Abuse & Religious Addiction (1994). Audio tapes to accompany book (see above).

Belonging: Healing & 12 Step Recovery (1992). Audio or videotapes and a course guide to accompany book (see above), for use as a program of recovery.

Healing the Eight Stages of Life (1991). Tapes and a course guide that can be used with book (see above) as a course in healing the life cycle. Available in video and audio versions.

Prayer Course for Healing Life's Hurts (1983). Ways to pray for personal healing that integrate physical, emotional, spiritual and social dimensions. Book includes course guide, and tapes are available in video and audio versions.

Praying with Another for Healing (1984). Guide to praying with another to heal hurts such as sexual abuse, depression, loss of a loved one, etc. Book includes course guide, and tapes are available in video and audio versions. *Healing the Greatest Hurt* (see above) may be used as supplementary reading for the last five of these sessions, which focus on healing of grief for the loss of a loved one.

Dying to Live: Healing through Jesus' Seven Last Words (with Bill & Jean Carr, 1983). How the seven last words of Jesus empower us to fully live the rest of our life. Tapes (available in video or audio versions) may be used with the book *Healing the Dying* (with Mary Jane Linn, 1979).

Audio tapes for all of these courses are available from Christian Video Library, 3914-A Michigan Ave., St. Louis, MO 63118, home (314) 865-0729, FAX (314) 773-3115. *Belonging* and *Good Goats* audio tapes are also available from Credence Cassettes, 115 E. Armour Blvd., Kansas City, MO 64111, (800) 444-8910.

Videotapes for all of these courses (except *Good Goats, Prayer Course for Healing Life's Hurts* and *Belonging*) are available from Christian Video Library (address and telephone above). *Good Goats* and *Prayer Course for Healing Life's Hurts* may be purchased from Paulist Press, 997 Macarthur Boulevard, Mahwah, NJ 07430, Phone orders (800) 218-1903, FAX orders (800) 836-3161. *Belonging* videotapes are available from Credence Cassettes (address and telephone above).

VIDEOTAPES ON A DONATION BASIS

To borrow any of the above videotapes, contact Christian Video Library (address and telephone above).

SPANISH BOOKS & TAPES

Several of the above books and tapes are available in Spanish. For information, contact Christian Video Library.

RETREATS & CONFERENCES

For retreats and conferences by the authors on the material in this book and related topics, and on other material in the resources listed above, contact
Dennis, Sheila & Matthew Linn, c/o Re-Member Ministries
3914-A Michigan Ave., St. Louis, MO 63118
Phone (970) 476-9235 or
(314) 865-0729
FAX (970) 476-9235 or
(314) 773-3115

ABOUT THE AUTHORS

Dennis, Sheila and Matt Linn work together as a team, integrating physical, emotional and spiritual wholeness, having worked as hospital chaplains and therapists, and currently in leading retreats and spiritual direction. They have taught courses on healing in over forty countries and in many universities, including a course to doctors accredited by the American Medical Association. Matt and Dennis are the co-authors of fourteen books, the last nine co-authored with Sheila. Their books include *Healing of Memories, Healing Life's Hurts* (revised 1993), *Healing the Dying* (with Sr. Mary Jane Linn), and *To Heal As Jesus Healed* (with Barbara Shlemon Ryan), *Prayer Course for Healing Life's Hurts, Praying with Another for Healing, Healing the Greatest Hurt, Healing the Eight Stages of Life, Belonging: Bonds of Healing & Recovery, Good Goats: Healing Our Image of God, Healing Spiritual Abuse & Religious Addiction* and *Sleeping with Bread: Holding What Gives You Life*. These books have sold over a million copies in English and have been translated into fifteen different languages.

ABOUT THE ILLUSTRATOR

Francisco Miranda lives in Mexico City. In addition to illustrating *Sleeping with Bread: Holding What Gives You Life, Good Goats: Healing Our Image of God* and *Healing Spiritual Abuse & Religious Addiction*, he has also written and illustrated several children's books.